DAILY
DECREES

for Government *and* Nations

DESTINY IMAGE BOOKS BY BRENDA KUNNEMAN

BRENDA KUNNEMAN

DAILY
DECREES

for Government *and* Nations

Raise Your Voice, Agree with Heaven,
and Shift Your Nation

DESTINY IMAGE® PUBLISHERS, INC.

PO Box 310, Shippensburg, PA 17257-0310

"Publishing cutting-edge prophetic resources to supernaturally empower the body of Christ"

This book and all other Destiny Image and Destiny Image Fiction books are available at Christian bookstores and distributors worldwide.

For more information on foreign distributors, call 717-532-3040.

Reach us on the Internet: www.destinyimage.com.

ISBN 13 TP: 9-780-7684-7202-8

ISBN 13 eBook: 9-780-7684-7203-5

For Worldwide Distribution, Printed in the USA

1 2 3 4 5 6 7 8 / 27 26 25 24 23

CONTENTS

FOREWORD

by Hank Kunneman

It is my honor to write this Foreword for my wife, Brenda, regarding *Daily Decrees for Government and Nations.* I have watched her dedication to praying, researching, and writing her many decree books under the inspiration of the Holy Spirit, especially this one. We are in a very important time not only in this nation, the United States, but all over the world as the Lord is awakening the nations to Him and pouring His glory upon all flesh. The unseen forces of darkness are aware of what has been promised in Scripture about the days that we live in, and through numerous avenues they are continuing to try and stop what God is doing. Many of those demonic assignments are clearly being seen in our government, media, education, curricula, attacks on our freedoms, elections that lack voter integrity, lies, deception, and evildoers rising to afflict hardships on the innocent. This is why we must be watchmen who don't just watch but do as Jesus instructed to both watch and pray. In these decrees, Brenda has given us a keen way to accomplish this by addressing many things we need to be aware of, and she powerfully equips us specifically on how to target our prayers more effectively.

As Joshua had a sword in his mouth to deliver a nation and people in the days of Israel, we have been handed a powerful tool to put in our hands and decree in our mouths to set the nations free. Brenda has an in-depth understanding that, when spoken, the power of the decree is as an arrow that becomes the arrow of deliverance with a release of the power of God upon the things being decreed. That power becomes manifested in the anointing of preservation. It preserves our freedoms, the people, governments, leaders, judges, society, education, entertainment, and the children from deception and the onslaught of the forces of darkness.

For years, Brenda has been writing decrees for our church to declare together, as well as for individuals to take and declare over their lives. As a church body, we have seen those things decreed come to pass, and as a ministry we have received powerful testimonies from those who have decreed and received God's hand moving in families, schools, children, finances, jobs, etc. When we decree with others in agreement with God and the powerful words in this book, the unified change it makes betters the lives of so many as well as the nations of this earth.

Brenda did not write this just to be a written book of decrees for governments and nations, but the very heart of God handed to us to be His extension in these perilous times that are filled with evil and those who cooperate with it. She has handed us a wakeup call for all who want to see God work a work in our day, as prophesied by the prophet Habakkuk—a work that is so good we won't even believe it. I encourage you to be the salt that preserves and heals the nations that have been wounded as the result of the lack of true justice and righteousness in our lands. I further exhort you to be the light, as Jesus mentioned, that doesn't just shine in the four walls of the church but shines into the darkness of the things happening in this hour. The decrees in this book will help you do just that; you will arise and shine causing God's light of truth to come and expose the darkness while establishing His righteousness upon the earth.

Aways be reminded that throughout Scripture, God did not avoid the subject of His Kingdom being involved in governments, leaders, society, education, children, and all other areas of the world influenced by evil. The pages in the Bible are filled with prophets, judges, and others who rise to the task of being used to affect change. We have examples of Noah, Abraham, Joseph, Moses, Daniel, the three Hebrew boys, Deborah,

Esther, and of course the many prophets who prophesied and decreed to affect change and be used as God's instruments to establish His Kingdom and the standard of what is right in the earth. We must also be reminded of those who came before us in the New Testament whose blood still speaks as a result of letting their lives make a difference by speaking up and acting boldly in the day they lived. In the same way, Brenda has given us decrees we can speak up and out with a boldness that will bring a rest to the nations and a change that will be celebrated throughout generations. We can carry the same pioneering spirit of Jesus, who was compared to John the Baptist and Elijah—nonconformists who spoke up and out to bring God's Kingdom standard to their nation and the people.

Lastly, we will be mentioned on the day we stand before our great God with others like Paul, Peter, and many in the early church and throughout modern history who stood up and spoke the Word of God in the face of those who led in governments and the very societies where they lived. It is my prayer that God will use these decrees through you to do the same. Decree a thing and it will be established (see Job 22:28). I encourage you to take these decrees and be that vessel of change who is forever remembered and honored by God Himself.

INTRODUCTION

Put simply, *Daily Decrees for Government and Nations* is meant to be a counterforce and a tool for God's Word to continue going forth in our nation freely and without censorship. It's a piece of equipment in the believer's prayer arsenal enabling them to pray prophetically and declare truth into the atmosphere. It is a series of faith declarations that not only builds our faith personally in fearful times but confronts the demons of darkness attempting to take over our nation and stop the work of the Gospel. Coupled with our duty as both citizens and Christians to be involved in civic issues, we must also lead the way in prayer and prophetic utterance. If we don't pray and prophesy hope over our nation, who will? The saints of God must be involved!

Recent times have brought up a fair amount of controversy over the matter of Christians being involved in the civic and political arena. We certainly see extremes on both sides; however, the greater extreme over the past several decades has truly existed on the side of Christians feeling they should stay out of political affairs, at least for the most part.

Most Christians do not mind voting during an election cycle or attending a constituents' prayer breakfast when it's in their interests to do so. Yet fewer believers and pastors want to throw themselves into the culture war over the declining moral issues facing our county. They don't want to enter a playing field where they can put up barriers to the false narratives and the extreme woke and antichrist ideologies being imposed upon society. That battle involves a much higher sacrifice and the potential for backlash increases exponentially; thus, many people shy away. Some also shy away because they feel speaking up is equated with being unloving, and the world is always ready to use this accusation to pressure us into silence. Yet rather than approach this dilemma biblically, many believers take the easy road of going along with the bully demands of secular critics and end up doing nothing at all.

It's important, however, to understand that the Bible has plenty to say about God's people being involved in civic and cultural matters. We cannot employ the weak argument that our nation is simply an earthly establishment that will one day be dissolved and therefore our only attention should be on God's heavenly Kingdom, abating all necessity to be involved in national issues. That sounds ideal at first glance, except that we live in a world where both the spiritual and natural realms collide. Yes, we wrestle not against flesh and blood, but let's face it, flesh and blood *will* be used by the demonic forces we are fighting, and we will have to interact with people while simultaneously waging war in the heavenlies.

This fact is true politically and culturally, and we will be forced to be involved, naturally speaking, at some point whether we want to or not. Avoiding social issues in the name of prioritizing the spiritual realm fails in multiple ways. It's like the schoolteacher saying they won't insert themselves to break up a fight on the playground because the battle is spiritual. We must realize that the hot button topics spread across our newspapers and television screens will touch us all on a personal level eventually, and believers and churches must have their position on these topics clearly injected into the conversation.

Consider that most of the prophets and Old Testament figures inserted themselves on a political level, acting as the force of resistance against the conduct of countless wicked kings and leaders. One of the greatest examples is the prophet Elijah and his constant run of interference against the evil deeds of Ahab and Jezebel. Moses stood up in the face of the political figure Pharoah and demanded liberty for a people.

Then consider how Jesus was an intercept to the political system and its moral corruption. If He wasn't a thorn in the government's side, they wouldn't have wanted Him dead or accused Him of defying the supremacy of Caesar himself. John the Baptist also confronted Herod and the *many* evils he had done (see Luke 3:19-20). The early apostles, including the apostle Paul, regularly flew in the face of political leaders, defying their threats and mandates to shut down the liberty of the Gospel.

Today, our fight in the various civic arenas is to be a counter assault to the advancement of darkness. We involve ourselves in the voting process lest it be led down the path to total evil, handing the leadership of our nation over to the vilest of individuals. We speak up on bills and initiatives, otherwise the pleasures of evildoers will become the normal way of life. We stand up for moral righteousness in our schools, capitals, and businesses because we aren't willing to let society fall unchallenged into the hands of demonically inspired agendas. As pastors, we stand in our church pulpits speaking about moral and civic issues because these issues *are* addressed in the Bible, and we want God's Word to have a place in society. Therefore, we will gladly assume our responsibility to ensure it.

Paul prayed that the Word of the Lord would have the unhindered ability to spread rapidly (see 2 Thess. 3:1). Yet if we don't stand up to the spirit of antichrist dominating much of the public and political culture, the spreading of God's Word will be hindered. We know that if left undisputed, there are those who would love nothing more than to close our churches, shut down our voices on the air, and deem the Bible another vehicle of misinformation. If we separate ourselves from the political culture war, content to keep our ministry to a select church audience without including what's happening in society, then that is exactly what they will do. They will *ensure* we are permanently removed from interfering, just like has happened in many socialist countries. It's already being attempted here in the United States on multiple fronts and it's time to sound the alarm.

One might retort and say, "Well, yes, but God's Word has continued to spread even in communist nations where people are unable to declare truth before their government." My counter is, yes of course, God's Word will never be completely stopped from going forth! However, it's better when it's being spread in a liberated environment or Paul wouldn't have prayed what he did. The Bible says that after Paul was saved and no longer imprisoning and killing Christians, the churches had rest (see Acts 9:31). The Bible mentions this because there are times of rest needed, without the constant onslaught, for God's Word to be the most effectual. Undoubtedly, Paul recognized this fact, and perhaps it was clear to him as he remembered how he was once the attacker against God's Word and how difficult he made things for the Church.

God knows there is the need for His work and His Word to be able to go forth without extreme government control and censorship. This precious liberty has been the characteristic of the United States. America has been the paramount country that has spread the Gospel worldwide, and for this reason God raised it up as a beacon of light. This nation has done more work globally for the Gospel than any other country, and God will defend this nation because of it. Can we imagine the souls unreached had this country been under communist control for these last two centuries? It's been our nation's unmatched freedom that has made the way in these end times for God's Word to impact the world. God is looking for the involvement of His people right now to keep the door open so that the Gospel can continue moving forward through America.

Notably, our patriotic allegiance to this nation is not to replace or somehow be equalized with the Kingdom of God. Our patriotism is because we love America and what she has stood for and the liberty that allows us to preach God's Word freely and openly. We love this country because it offers life, liberty, and the pursuit of happiness in a similar manner that Jesus expressed when He said, *"I have come to give you life and life more abundantly"* (see John 10:10).

We support and rally behind political figures who stand for our values, not because we idolize them. Instead, we appreciate that they are standing up against the evil that is trying to destroy everything this nation has offered as a conduit for the Gospel around the world. We know that the right leaders in office will be a hurdle in front of the onslaught of evil that utterly hates the God we serve.

My prayer is that *Daily Decrees for Government and Nations* will be a prayer tool in your hands because we desperately need intercessors who are praying for our country. But I also pray the words contained in these prayers and exhortations will ignite a fire within you. The words inscribed in this book are unfiltered, bold in nature, and designed to confront and expose the hidden evils coming against the United States. To the best of my ability, I have attempted to leave no key topic on the shelf, but rather bring it out in the open and address it with biblical truth in a statesmanlike manner. I pray this book will help you pray for America with confidence and cause a holy boldness against the demons of darkness to arise within you! I pray it gives you hope that we *can* each do something to enforce a divine change.

Perhaps you are reading this book and are from another country, believing and praying for a divine turnaround where you live. Please use these decrees and replace the mention of America with your own country! Through civic involvement along with our bold prophetic prayers and decrees, we shall surely see this nation and the nations of the earth become better, and God's power shall be witnessed in our land and around the world!

A NATION OF REVIVAL!

DECLARATION

We declare the United States of America shall experience revival! We speak that there shall be an awakening that shall blanket this land. We call upon the Lord of Heaven's Armies to turn the hearts of men away from evil and toward righteousness. We speak that there shall be a move of God that shall permeate society, our cities, and our governments. We declare the powers of evil are bound from their wicked agenda to promote moral decay, violence, and sin. We decree there shall be a return to the house of God, and families shall once again call upon the Name of the Lord. We say there shall be a revival of the Holy Spirit's power that shall bring deliverance, healing, and salvation! We decree that America is a nation of revival, and we declare America shall be saved! Amen!

SCRIPTURE

Revive us so we can call on your name once more.
Turn us again to yourself, O Lord God of Heaven's

*Armies. Make your face shine down upon us. Only
then will we be saved* (Psalm 80:18-19 NLT).

WORD OF ENCOURAGEMENT

Revival is a word used often in Christendom and is something that every true believer wants to see happen. We
want to see masses of people saved and for backslidden
believers to turn back to God. But to experience this,
of course it begins with us personally. We first need to
examine the areas of our own lives and be willing to make
adjustments, so we aren't contributing to the larger prob-
lem happening on a mass scale. Are we living for God
wholeheartedly? Are we attending church and walking
righteously and so forth? Undoubtedly, believers who
are passionately on fire for God will work to be part of
the solution. They will influence others to walk in biblical righteousness because they walk that way. They will
encourage others to be committed to church because they
are committed. They will set the example of bringing the
Gospel to a place of prominence in the public square.

The second important element for national revival is
to have faith for it. We can't just throw up our hands at the
evil all around and say, "What's the use? There's no hope!"

Our Scripture expresses a tone of expectancy for revival and a national awakening. It's a direct appeal to God that expresses faith for an answer. It even adds a warfare element to it through the mention of Heaven's armies being involved. In other words, the desire is for God to conduct spiritual warfare through His people so the enemy's plans will be interrupted and cause the nation to turn around. As we pray for revival, we must also decree as though it is going to undoubtedly happen! We need to envision a massive awakening regardless of the evidence of evil. We need to decree revival is here! Let's call our nation a nation of revival!

CENSORSHIP OF THE GOSPEL INTERRUPTED

DECLARATION

We declare that the Word of God shall have the freedom in our society to be spoken and distributed without resistance, persecution, or censorship. We prophesy that the Word of the Lord and the Gospel shall not return void, but it shall accomplish everything it has been sent to do. We command all demonic operations that would rise to withstand the Word of God to be bound in the Name of Jesus! We speak a breaking apart of the forces that would censor, cancel, ban, and delete the truth, and we say they are rendered ineffective. We say that God's Word and the truth shall be promoted, shared, platformed, and it shall fill the airwaves! May the pulpits and people of this nation who are declaring and standing for truth be given their rightful place of prominence. We decree that all censoring and restriction against the truth shall be interrupted and halted in Jesus' Name!

SCRIPTURE

Finally, brethren, pray for us, that the word of the Lord may have free course, and be glorified, even as it is with you (2 Thessalonians 3:1 KJV).

WORD OF ENCOURAGEMENT

If there is one thing that we have learned in recent times is that the voice of truth and God's Word has been censored and restricted online in a greater way than we had previously imagined. For the most part, citizens of the United States have enjoyed the liberty to worship freely, promote God's Word, and live openly as believers. Then it became clear along the way that certain groups were determined to ensure that our messages of truth, whether it be God's Word or truth regarding issues in society, were not going to be easily welcomed. Extensive measures were taken to prevent our messages from being shared. However, censorship of the Gospel and truth is nothing new. When Peter and John offered healing to the man at the Gate Beautiful, they were vehemently resisted and unjustly arrested for preaching the truth (see Acts 3–4). But the more governmental leaders attempted to silence them, the more bold and determined they became. Then we find through the rest of the Book of Acts that not only did the censorship against the early church fail, but the Word of God also grew mightily!

What we must remember in this current season of cancel culture, banning, and deleting is that truth will never be stopped no matter how hard some try. Like the early apostles, we need a greater boldness to keep using every means we have to spread the Gospel, speak the truth, and stand for what is right. We must also pray like the early church, who asked God to look upon their threats, clear the way for them through supernatural means, and grant them more boldness in their ability to take a stand (see Acts 4:29). When we call out to God, what they try to silence will be shouted on the housetops. What they have tried to censor shall be interrupted in Jesus' Name!

DELIVERED FROM WICKED AND EVIL PEOPLE

DECLARATION

We decree deliverance from every attack that would be attempted from violent, irrational, and unreasonable people. We say no assailant can succeed in any form of physical or verbal assault. We break the power of every attacker, raider, intruder, liar, accuser, persecutor, or evil antagonist in the Name of Jesus! We declare they cannot enact violence against us for our faith, our message, or our stand for truth. We prophesy that no weapon formed against us can prosper because the angels of the Lord stand watch to protect us from evil. We speak protection over our loved ones and our property. We plead the blood of Jesus upon our lives to save us in every situation and to prevent the workers of darkness from any scheme that would steal our peace. We prophesy deliverance, escape, and rescue by the hand of the Lord against every wicked snare. We say deliverance rests upon us, upon our families, our homes and communities, and we live in peace and safety in Jesus' Name!

SCRIPTURE

Finally, brethren, pray for us, that the word of the Lord may have free course, and be glorified, even as it is with you: and that we may be delivered from unreasonable and wicked men: for all men have not faith (2 Thessalonians 3:1-2 KJV).

Deliver me, O Lord, from the evil man: preserve me from the violent man (Psalm 140:1 KJV).

WORD OF ENCOURAGEMENT

In the verses above, when Paul requested prayer to escape the attacks of violent and unreasonable people, we gain a clear understanding that there are those who will go to all lengths in order to attempt an attack on the Gospel. Notably, when Paul used the adjective "unreasonable" he was outlining the fact that there are people who are so irrational that there is nothing you can naturally do to mitigate their attacks. They are so full of demonic influence that it requires God's supernatural hand to stop them. As the last days continue to escalate, we must use our faith and call upon God to intervene and keep us from the aggression of evildoers. We must know undoubtedly that God is able and willing to respond when we call upon His angelic forces. We have to build our assurance that God is our defense according to the Scripture that says, "*The Lord is my helper, and I will not fear what man shall do unto me*" (Heb. 13:6 KJV). Stand confidently today that God is faithful and will deliver you from those who are wicked and unreasonable!

DECLARATION OVER THE OFFICE OF THE PRESIDENT

DECLARATION

We decree God's hand to rest upon our duly elected president who has been placed in office through fair and honest elections. We speak that the hand of the Lord shall lead and guide the president to make quality decisions in accordance with the Constitution of the United States. We prophesy that no fraud, deception, scheme, or plot can prevent the rightful president from holding office. We say that the president shall be one who follows biblical and moral values and stands for truth and integrity. We decree our president shall defend life, traditional marriage, and be a defender of the Church and the Gospel. We declare that no liar, deceiver, evildoer, traitor, or thief shall hold the office, in Jesus' Name. We prophesy that the president shall love and defend America, its citizens, and its interests around the globe. Our president shall defend and support Israel. We say that our president shall surround themselves with wise counsel, godly advisors, and trustworthy allies. We declare the president shall have favor with God and man, conducting foreign affairs with wisdom and prudence. The president shall be a peacemaker, but shall stand up against terrorism and invasions, both foreign and domestic. We call upon God to direct our president to undergird our men and women in uniform and maintain a strong and stable military. We decree the president of the United States of America shall benefit this land and work for the interests of the people in Jesus' Name, Amen!

SCRIPTURE

> *I exhort therefore, that, first of all, supplications, prayers, intercessions, and giving of thanks, be made for all men; for kings, and for all that are in authority; that we may lead a quiet and peaceable life in all godliness and honesty* (1 Timothy 2:1-2 KJV).

WORD OF ENCOURAGEMENT

This declaration over the president truly speaks for itself, and many things even beyond this could be prayed for and declared over the highest office of the land. That said, it's easy for everyone to have their varying opinions of what a president should do, look like, and how they should behave. But the most important prayer we should pray is that our president will defend the biblical values that we as believers hold dear. While it's probably unrealistic to think that most presidents will be among the most committed of Christians, we can certainly expect that our president will uphold a basic moral code and standard that does not undermine the Christian heritage that our nation was founded upon. We can ask God to give us presidents who do not defy and interfere with the work of the Church nationwide and who value our country's godly foundation. When these basics are in order, the other necessary elements that surround the office will follow. Declare for God's person to be put in place so the sanctity of our nation will be maintained. When we do so, the Bible reminds us it will lead to a quiet and peaceable life!

A "Put It Back!" Movement

DECLARATION

We decree that there shall be a "put it back" movement that shall blanket this land, and people everywhere shall demand the foundations that have been unjustly removed be put back into place. Where our nation's foundational and biblical values have been torn down, they shall be put back! We prophesy that morality shall be put back, prayer in schools shall be put back, and principles of integrity shall return. Decency, peace, and manners shall arise within the culture as people everywhere call for a restoration of the respectable virtues established by our forefathers. We speak that the evil ideologies of wokeism, liberal progressivism, socialism, and all communistic belief systems shall be exposed by the truth and shunned in society. We declare the right to free speech shall no longer be infringed upon, and the truth of our nation's history shall be taught and upheld in our schools and universities. We call for a clear return to the upholding of the Constitution in our courts and within the executive, judicial, and legislative branches of government.

We say the honor of the Bible shall be put back in the public square and seen within the framework of society. We prophesy a pushback against evil that will lead to a "put it back" movement in this land in Jesus' Name!

SCRIPTURE

> *And I will bring again the captivity of my people of Israel, and they shall build the waste cities, and inhabit them; and they shall plant vineyards, and drink the wine thereof; they shall also make gardens, and eat the fruit of them* (Amos 9:14 KJV).

WORD OF ENCOURAGEMENT

One of the most exciting things we have seen in recent times is certain elements in society where good has been removed and then put back into place. Things such as prayer being removed from schools and in most forms of public address are now making a comeback. People are beginning to honor God in places where they were told it wasn't allowed. Historical monuments that were torn down are being rebuilt. God has been showing us that there is truly a pushback against so many of the wicked agendas. People are rising up with a determination to say, "Enough is enough!"

It's important that we do not assume once something has seemingly been revoked that it's gone forever. For example, consider how many countries or regions throughout history that have been under some form of tyranny were suddenly liberated. Many believers have looked at the good, godliness, and morals that have been removed in our nation and have given up pursuing a restoration of such things. Yet history reminds us to never give up! Countless documentations reveal that when it seemed all hope was lost, ultimately a pushback arose that resulted in a putting back of good and betterment for the people. Keep standing in faith today because God is restoring things lost in our nation as people everywhere demand, "Put it back!"

ECONOMIC BLESSING AND PROVISION

DECLARATION

We decree that the economy of this nation shall return to and remain in the place of stability and strength. We prophesy that our currency and markets shall maintain their highest value. We command all demonic forces of poverty, debt, lack, and shortage to be bound from wreaking havoc on our national wealth in Jesus' Name. We call for the reduction of the national deficit. We break the power of out-of-control inflation and price gouging and declare its sting against our citizens' well-being is rendered powerless. In the Name of Jesus, we break the power of the waster, the plunderer, and all who would immorally abuse and misuse funds. We prophesy that all bills, legislation, and laws that allow pork barrel spending by the government to be overthrown! We say that funding directed toward wicked special interests and foreign enemies shall be halted. Our tax dollars shall be used to fund life, not death, and education over indoctrination! We declare that godly and wise overseers and experts shall be positioned over the nation's budgets and spending. We speak that the states, cities, and municipalities shall manage their financial affairs with integrity, prudence, and discretion. We declare that the government shall always financially undergird and provide relief to the work of the Lord's Church. We decree the people of this nation shall be fed and provided for and this economy shall be characterized by stability and the Lord's blessing!

SCRIPTURE

When there is moral rot within a nation, its government topples easily. But wise and knowledgeable leaders bring stability (Proverbs 28:2 NLT).

WORD OF ENCOURAGEMENT

The economy is a topic that is always on the minds of Americans, and it's always at the forefront of discussion during every election cycle. What happens with the national economy affects every individual, household, and business. People's well-being is highly connected to economic conditions. This begs us as believers to make it a key matter of prayer and bold declaration. While in the natural it can be frustrating at times that we don't feel we can control how the government often foolishly spends our hard-earned tax dollars, we need to resist the temptation to just gripe and complain like so many do. We need to use our spiritual authority in prayer to create a shift in the economic downturn and immoral actions of politicians who bring rot to our financial stability. We can pray for God to establish wise leadership that will restore and maintain our nation's financial health. It's also important to note the good our country has done in how the poor and destitute around the world have been helped by America's wealth. Some at the hand of government programs, yes, but also through the work of the Church via missions and relief programs worldwide. The Bible says that he who gives to the poor lends to the Lord and will be repaid (see Prov. 19:17). God is still looking at the good this nation has done and is blessing us for it. But remember, your prayers and declarations over the economy are key to seeing it stay in a place of stability!

INTEGRITY IN ELECTIONS

DECLARATION

We decree that the United States of America shall be marked by election integrity. Our republic shall be known for laws and legislation that shall protect the democratic process and the right of every citizen to vote and have their vote counted fairly and honestly. We break the power of the thief and the deceiver, and we say that their schemes and plans to manipulate votes shall be exposed in the Name of Jesus! We say that each state shall enact laws to protect its elections from being interfered with by criminal activity. We declare that the courts shall be committed to try and prosecute election fraud. We prophesy that foreign entities shall be stopped from having access to our elections, voting methods, and candidates. We declare that no illegal person's vote or illegitimate votes shall be counted. We bind the work of violence from arising against the true will of the people regarding their votes, in Jesus' Name. We decree that candidates shall arise who will uphold their oaths to work by and for the people, and they shall maintain their offices in truth and integrity. We say that the voters across this nation shall vote en masse to uphold morality, life, biblical values, and decency and that all ballot agendas to further evil in the culture shall be discarded and unable to succeed. We decree that no judge or candidate shall be fraudulently inserted or inaugurated in Jesus' mighty Name! We say integrity covers our nation's elections!

SCRIPTURE

Do not steal. Do not deceive or cheat one another (Leviticus 19:11 NLT).

Make your motions and cast your votes, but God has the final say (Proverbs 16:33 MSG).

WORD OF ENCOURAGEMENT

The controversy over election integrity has saturated every recent election and there have been clear and obvious reasons why this issue concerns voters. One of the most sacred rights of any citizen is to make their voice heard through the casting of their ballots. To realize that one's rights were taken away by fraud is not only infuriating but unacceptable. As bearers of the truth, every Christian should be among the most outspoken about any hint of election fraud across the board and not be willing to sweep evidence of such under the rug. To believe widespread fraud isn't a reality when clear evidence suggests otherwise is to truly aid the furtherance of a lie. To avoid even looking at evidence is no different. We as believers should be adamant against turning a blind eye to the truth. In fact, we are the bearers of the truth and should be the ones who set the standard for upholding it.

Of course, because of issues such as election fraud coupled with candidates who seem to have compromised values, many believers have taken themselves from the political conversation and determined not to bother voting. However, that approach fixes nothing and only allows evil to go on unchecked. Our nation was built on a fair electoral process, and we must cherish and protect it. Declare in faith for fair and honest elections!

JUDGES OF RIGHTEOUSNESS

DECLARATION

We decree that our nation shall have judges of righteousness! They shall work to uphold the rule of law with integrity and honor. We prophesy that judges who are committed to that which is truthful and right shall be positioned, anointed, and appointed, and those who would rule in wickedness shall be removed from office. Our judges shall be dedicated to protecting truth and morality. We prophesy that our judges on every level, local, district, federal, and even on the highest court, shall rule in righteousness and without fear. We bind the workers of violence from intimidating and bullying righteous judges. We speak a failure to the attempts of every attacker, vandal, murderer, stalker, and false accuser who would arise against righteous judges. We break the power of lying, manipulation, evasion, and tactics of delay that would prevent the appropriate cases from being heard and right rulings from being decided and adjudged in Jesus' Name. We declare judges shall be appointed who shall not exploit their office nor legislate from the bench. We say the juries of our land shall arbitrate in truth and according to sound justice, and fair and honest legal cases, lawsuits, and trials shall mark our nation's courts. We decree honorable judges shall arise in the United States of America! In Jesus' Name, amen!

SCRIPTURE

Thus speaketh the Lord of hosts, saying, Execute true judgment, and shew mercy and compassions every man to his brother (Zechariah 7:9 KJV). *And I will restore thy judges as at the first, and thy counsellors as at the beginning: afterward thou shalt be called, The city of righteousness, the faithful city* (Isaiah 1:26 KJV).

WORD OF ENCOURAGEMENT

One of the most important prayers believers can pray when it comes to their nation is that honorable and righteous judges will be placed in office. We know how detrimental the wrong judge can be. In fact, Jesus talked about the unjust judge whose hardness of heart, for a time, kept him from even hearing the case of a desperate widow who was clearly being abused by an enemy (see Luke 18:1-6). The Bible says this judge did not fear God and he couldn't care less about the plight of anyone in his district. From the biblical account, it sounds like he was one who even refused to hear legitimate cases brought to his court whenever it was in his selfish interest to do so. And if this was anything like today, I am sure this judge had a reputation in the community. Undoubtedly people were shocked when he refused certain cases in which clear evidence was presented and which should have been heard. We see many such judges today, many whose agenda is to obstruct the Gospel and righteousness.

But the good news is that God on many accounts promised that He will cause righteous judges to be placed. We must ask the Lord to position them so this next season can bring peace to the land and allow the work of the Lord to prosper and prevail! Let's call on Heaven for righteous judges!

HEAVENLY PERSPECTIVE UPON THE NATION

DECLARATION

We decree that the people and believers of the United States shall receive divine revelation and Heaven's perspective. We prophesy that the citizens of this country shall hear and know the truth. In Jesus' Name, we say they shall not be dissuaded by the lies perpetrated through the media, political figures, activists, and special interests. We bind the work of the god of this world who would blind their minds and keep the light the Gospel from shining unto them. We declare that those who resist and refuse the truth shall lose their influence and be exposed in their deceptions. We call for opening the eyes and ears of every person, family, Christian, community leader, and political figure. We say they are open to what God is saying in this hour. We prophesy that biblical truth and prophetic insight shall be welcomed in people's hearts and minds. We decree a new perspective about the future shall arise and this nation shall clearly see God's redemptive plan of good that is being extended to humanity. Men and women everywhere shall herald and promote God's Word of life. We decree people shall turn to God and to His perspective in all things, and Heaven's perspective shall mightily prevail, in Jesus' Name!

SCRIPTURE

> *In whom the god of this world hath blinded the minds of them which believe not, lest the light of the glorious gospel of Christ, who is the image of God, should shine unto them* (2 Corinthians 4:4 KJV).

WORD OF ENCOURAGEMENT

I am sure you can agree that a whole lot would be different in the world if more people could take on God's perspective on things. Even a number of believers today have lost the connection to God's will and intent when it comes to His purposes for the nation or even humanity itself. Many have simply taken on perspectives presented by the media and also from ungodly personalities whom they deem to be experts on various things. They also build perspectives based on their own personal belief systems. Some are biased in believing that during the end times, everything will continue to spiral downward, and so all they can emphasize is a gloomy future.

Yet what we must remember is that all throughout history, during the darkest of times, God always had a redemptive plan amidst the darkness, which is a plan of help and hope. Getting God's perspective begins first with us as Christians. We have to be able to see what God is doing during dark times, and that He always has a plan to bless and offer hope. Second, we need to pray that those who don't even know the Lord will come to the revelation of the truth. Yes, truth that causes them to come to salvation, but also truth about society and cultural issues at hand that will lead to salvation. We have seen in recent times even many unsaved media personalities, celebrities, athletes, and the like beginning to take on a perspective of truth in the middle of a sea of lies. The Bible is clear that it's the God of this world who blinds the minds of unbelievers to try and prevent them from receiving truth. We need to pray and command those blinders to come down so they will see God's heavenly perspective!

We the People *of the United States, in order to form a more perfect Union, establish Justice, insure domestic Tranquility, provide for the common defence, promote the general Welfare, and secure the Blessings of Liberty to ourselves and our Posterity, do ordain and establish this Constitution for the United States of America.*

Article I   Article II

LIBERTY PROTECTED

DECLARATION

We decree this nation shall be one that is marked by liberty and freedom for the people! We prophesy that the privileges established in our Constitution for the right to life, liberty, and the pursuit of happiness shall be preserved. We break the power of all governmental ideologies that would attempt to place a chokehold on the joyous freedoms this nation was founded upon. We bind the work of socialism, communism, totalitarianism, and Marxism from gaining ground in our country, in Jesus' Name! We declare that capitalism, free enterprise, and industrialism shall stand strong in society and shall prosper. We prophesy that our nation shall defend the right for the Church of the Lord Jesus Christ to have its rightful place in the public square and in the political arena. We say nothing shall infringe upon the right we have to gather in our homes, churches, or in public places, and we shall always be able to worship freely. The preaching of the Bible shall not be infringed upon, and the pulpits of America shall remain free from all laws that would bind their voice to speak and preach God's Word without restriction. We declare the liberty of the United States of America shall be protected in the Name of Jesus! Amen!

SCRIPTURE

For, brethren, ye have been called unto liberty; only use not liberty for an occasion to the flesh, but by love serve one another (Galatians 5:13 KJV).

WORD OF ENCOURAGEMENT

One of the marks of God's character is that He wants people free—free to live a fulfilled and abundant life. He did not create human beings for them to be bound and chained, whether it be spiritually, emotionally, physically or culturally. Tyranny and governmental control that keeps its citizens beholden to laws that inflict harm are something God is adamantly against. One of the key reasons, among others, that God has blessed our nation is because it was established to promote liberty, specifically the liberty to worship the Lord and honor Him freely. And yes, while God is the author of freedom, we know that freedom should never be interpreted as a free-for-all to commit wrong and evil (see Gal. 5:13).

That said, there are always those lurking who would love to take the orderly experience and meaning of liberty away. The devil is the author of bondage and control, and he is always working to steal our freedoms. He will definitely try to do that with people personally, keeping them bound to certain things, or he will attempt it in society and in the nation as well. We have already witnessed how liberal progressives and those bent upon socialist ideologies want to impose their philosophies on the rest of society and remove all sense of free enterprise, making most things state and government owned and regulated. History clearly reveals the evil that always ensues under this type of government. We need to continue to pray and declare that the liberties and freedoms that this nation was founded upon and the freedom given the Church shall always be protected!

PEACE AND SAFETY

DECLARATION

We decree that the citizens of this land shall live in safety, without being overshadowed by dread and fear. We say that this country shall be known as a place where its citizens are able to exist in a society not marked by crime, violence, terrorism, or political unrest. They are able to conduct business and enjoy life without threat. We declare that this land shall be surrounded in peace and the Lord's protection. We say that foreign enemies, invaders, cartels, gangs, and mobs shall not plunder our borders, cities, states, and regions. We declare that riots, brawls, shootings, and lawless protests shall not rob the tranquility of our streets and neighborhoods, in Jesus' Name! We prophesy that people shall be able to live in their homes without fear of burglary and invasion. May the hand of the Lord still the agenda of the violent and release a spirit of peace upon our land. We declare our nation shall not be overcome by destruction, natural disaster, violent weather, and tragic events. We decree peace and safety over our nation in Jesus' Name!

SCRIPTURE

And they shall dwell safely therein, and shall build houses, and plant vineyards; yea, they shall dwell with confidence, when I have executed judgments upon all those that despise them round about them; and they shall know that I am the Lord their God (Ezekiel 28:26 KJV).

WORD OF ENCOURAGEMENT

When the blessing of the Lord is upon a nation, you typically see that it is largely marked by an overall peace and order. It's not engulfed in ongoing mass violence, tragedy, and mayhem. People can normally conduct themselves without a constant sense of dread. While no country is without moments of outburst by those with wicked intentions, it shouldn't be a widespread or a constant occurrence. Evildoers will always be in the world, but our prayers and decrees are part of the solution to repel the work of terror from being unleashed. The United States has largely afforded its citizens the ability and opportunity to live in peace and safety. While not without some obvious incidents of tragedy, we have typically been viewed as a country of order in the broad sense of the word. However, as the last days continue to escalate and the signs the Bible describes continue to unfold worldwide, we need to be decreeing even more that our nation is marked by an overall peace and safety. I believe our prayers and declarations can interrupt the plans of the enemy that would desire to unleash a spirit of chaos and terror. And we should not think that just because it is the last days we can't do anything to interrupt the darkness! God doesn't stop moving in His power because we are approaching the end times. We, the Church, have a job to do in prayer to disrupt evil and call upon Heaven to rain down peace and safety upon us! We must prophesy that the United States of America is a nation of tranquility and peace!

LIFE FOR THE UNBORN!

DECLARATION

We decree that this nation defends the right to life for the unborn! We prophesy an awakening that will turn people's hearts to the truth regarding children in the womb. We say they shall see that life begins at conception and that the Lord knew us before we were formed in our mother's belly. May each pregnant mother receive a divine understanding of the value of her child and that her children have a purpose and calling. May the fathers of each child encourage mothers to choose life. We declare that laws shall be enacted in each state and province that defend the right to life. We say that the voices of those who stand for life shall be heard and received. We break the power of the murderous spirit of abortion in the United States of America. We command the demonic influence of the ancient spirit of Molech to be torn down in the Name of Jesus! May the attempts of every political figure, organization, and activist who would promote lies about abortion be exposed and halted. We cry out against the aborting of our children in this land,

and we speak and decree life for the unborn, in Jesus' Name!

SCRIPTURE

Today I have given you the choice between life and death, between blessings and curses. Now I call on Heaven and earth to witness the choice you make. Oh, that you would choose life, so that you and your descendants might live! (Deuteronomy 30:19 NLT)

WORD OF ENCOURAGEMENT

The topic of abortion remains a paramount subject when it comes to praying for nations and government and is a top campaign issue in every election. The battle rages on just as intensely as when Roe v. Wade was first ruled upon over 50 years ago. Reasonable people, who in some cases don't even claim to be Christian, recognize the cruel nature of abortion. It's impossible to ignore the horror of the abortion process with its barbaric and demonic complexion. We can't soften to the fact that abortion is inspired by hell itself, and the same ancient demons who used political figures in the Bible to murder children are still using people today for this wicked practice.

The Bible is clear that abortion is murder, even though some deceptively try to assert the opposite by twisting Scripture to try and herald a pro-choice view. Yet they can't ignore how the Bible details that God knitted us together in our mother's womb (see Ps. 139:13-16), and then He named us and called us before the day of our birth (see Isa. 49:1; Jer. 1:5). And of course, the Bible is clear that we must never commit murder, and there is simply no way to call abortion anything less. We can go on to emphasize how John the Baptist, while still inside his mother Elizabeth, leapt for joy when she greeted Mary (see Luke 1:41). Abortion advocates have to deliberately ignore that the child inside her was a human being with feelings and emotions! As believers, we must not let off the gas in the fight against the evil that abortion is, and we must continually pray and declare life for the unborn!

Weye People

LIARS AND DECEIVERS
EXPOSED!

DECLARATION

We decree that the liars who deceive and mislead the people of this nation shall be exposed for their crooked ways. We prophesy that they shall repent of their deeds that have been crafted in covert darkness to commit harm. We say that which has been done wickedly in secret shall be shouted upon the housetops. That which has been hidden shall be brought to light. Those who cause the innocent to stumble and fall shall be brought to justice and no longer be able to further their treacherous lies. We bind the demons of lying, deceit, fraud, trickery, and hypocrisy in Jesus' Name! We command truth to prevail upon our land. We speak that lies perpetrated on the airways shall be exposed, and we loose the spirit of truth. We prophesy that media outlets that are committed to truth shall arise and defy the false. May the people of this nation see through every lying spirit and embrace truthful facts. We say that liars and deceivers shall be exposed, in Jesus' Name!

SCRIPTURE

People with integrity walk safely, but those who follow crooked paths will be exposed (Proverbs 10:9 NLT).

WORD OF ENCOURAGEMENT

A lying spirit that is determined to deceive and mislead is obviously a large contributor to what causes nations to crumble and fall. There is reason the term *propaganda* gets used so often. It's because people recognize that there are those who control communications for manipulative reasons. They want to further false narratives on a mass scale. Our job as believers in prayer is to loose the spirit of truth and command the demonic activity that furthers lies and deception to be bound in the Name of Jesus. We can also pray that liars and their lies will be exposed for what they truly are. We can pray they will be not only be exposed but unable to cause further harm upon innocent lives.

One thing we can rest assured about is that God will always have truth bearers in every season and generation. What we must do is determine to become one of those who bear and promote the truth, not only regarding the Gospel itself but regarding issues in society and culture. We must speak truth regarding biblical values and moral issues. We also can't shy away from speaking truth because of intimidation and fear. If we will not stand up and speak truth in what seems a sea of lies, then the lies can continue unhindered. Sure, standing up for what is right isn't always an easy task, and that is why prayer along these lines is so important. We can pray for God to help us, defend us, and expose those who spread lies. We can ask the Holy Spirit of Truth to guide and lead our hearts and the hearts of others toward truth and honesty. Our nation desperately needs us to pray and decree that the liars who aim to bring harm will lose their power, and truth will prevail and reign supreme!

GREAT GRACE UPON THE CHURCH

DECLARATION

We decree that the Church of the Lord in this nation shall be covered in great grace. With great power, it shall fulfill its mandate to preach, teach, witness, and declare righteousness and salvation across this land. We prophesy that a spirit of boldness rests upon the servants of God to speak God's Word. May the Lord's Church be marked by the manifestation of signs, wonders, miracles, and the supernatural gifts of the Spirit. May the mouths of God's people be filled with words of wisdom from the Holy Spirit. May our speech not be with the enticing words of human wisdom but in demonstration and power. We break a spirit of fear and intimidation from the Body of Christ. We say that God's people shall confidently obey God rather than comply with the pressure from the spirit of antichrist in the culture. In Jesus' Name, we declare that no weapon formed against the people of God can prosper! Every lying and accusing tongue that would spew hate against the Lord's Church shall fail and be condemned. We release a fresh anointing upon the houses of worship. We speak divine strength upon the pastors, leaders, prophets, and congregations that they shall not grow weary in well doing. We decree that in this season the Church of the Lord Jesus shall arise in prominence and take its rightful place in government, culture, and society. We declare great grace upon the Church!

SCRIPTURE

And with great power gave the apostles witness of the resurrection of the Lord Jesus: and great grace was upon them all (Acts 4:33 KJV).

WORD OF ENCOURAGEMENT

Just after the Day of Pentecost, the early apostles went forth preaching and demonstrating the Gospel, and their message was marked by great power and miracles. However, they immediately received pushback from the religious establishment of the day as well as the culture in general. They had an instant decision to make. Would they comply with the demands of their opposers to silence their message, or would they continue in their God-given assignment? The Bible certainly teaches us to be law abiding when it comes to basic moral and civil law that aims to instill decency and order in society. However, there comes a point when man-made laws and agendas oppose our calling to fulfill the Great Commission and abide by biblical truth and values. We are then required to stand by God and His commandments. Yes, it might create conflict and cause persecution, but like the early church we will have to determine to obey God rather than men. Yet we also learn that when the early church took its rightful stand, God backed them with great grace and power. Sure, their message wasn't always popular, but God intervened with miracles, deliverance, and supernatural manifestation. The Holy Spirit gave them the inner strength to stand in their calling and not be intimidated. God is releasing a fresh outpouring of great grace and power upon us in this season so we can be the glorious Church in this nation and impact the world!

GODLY LEADERS AND
INFLUENCERS EXALTED

DECLARATION

We decree that godly leaders shall arise in the United States of America. We prophesy that those in high offices of government and places of influence shall carry a righteous standard. We declare that Christ-like believers shall be positioned, established, and voted into government. We speak that they shall be well received, respected, and their offices honored by society and the culture. We declare that notable influencers in society shall carry a moral and biblical standard. We say the leaders and councilmembers in our cities, schools, and universities shall stand for that which is right and reject every antichrist agenda. We say that godly leaders, government officials, and influencers shall carry a righteous discernment and surround themselves with wise and moral counsel. In Jesus' Name, we break the power and influence of the godless and wicked rulers, activists, judges, journalists, professors, teachers, and businesses that seek to turn the minds of the culture toward evil. We say that the positional authority and thrones of the wicked shall crumble and fall. May they be removed from their places of influence and lose their ability to beguile, abuse, and mislead the citizens of this nation. We prophesy that across this land, in all sectors of society, godly leaders and people of influence shall arise and be exalted and our nation shall rejoice!

SCRIPTURE

A just king gives stability to his nation, but one who demands bribes destroys it (Proverbs 29:4 NLT).

It is an abomination to kings to commit wickedness: for the throne is established by righteousness (Proverb 16:12 KJV).

WORD OF ENCOURAGEMENT

Power in the wrong hands is destructive, tearing apart all soundness of life. Consider the effect that the lies and abuses of wicked governments and leaders have had on society over the years. It has inflicted a devastating moral decay in our educational systems, upon healthcare, business, entertainment, and upon nearly every other sector. It's also rendered a dismantling of the family structure. But consider when godly and morally upright governors and leaders are in power. We typically see health return to the economy, stability in our national security, and our constitutional rights protected. We see the people achieve prosperity and receive fair and just benefits. We also see liberty for the Church to advance the Gospel and moral values, unrestricted and uncensored!

However, some believers are afraid to pray that godless authorities will lose their power. They often quote Romans 13:1, which states that we are to be subject to governmental authority and that it's God who raises up such powers. However, we must examine the full context of this chapter, which speaks of the type of leader who is a "minister for good" and whose intent is to create reasonable social order for citizens to follow. The context is not speaking of unequivocally honoring leaders who impose an immoral, tyrannical agenda; otherwise, the early apostles who defied such governors and magistrates throughout the Book of Acts were in error. The truth that believers must obey civil law does not insinuate blind obedience to laws or mandates devised by evil, nor does it suggest that wicked, dishonest leaders should receive our undivided support. Such thinking insinuates that it's God who installs the most vicious dictators and expects His people to honor them. This simply isn't true. Remember, it's typically people who make way for wicked rulers, which God may at times allow, and Scripture reveals such. But Scripture also reveals the benefit and blessing when good leaders are positioned. Therefore, it's our calling to pray that wicked leaders won't be elected and shall be removed from office while the godly are exalted!

Truth and Business Integrity Prevails!

We decree that this nation shall be marked by business-people who walk uprightly and who speak truthfully. We say that integrity shall prevail nationwide in businesses, in our centers of research, in financial institutions, media outlets, systems of education, and offices of government. In Jesus' Name, we bind the power of shady deals, skewed reporting, mismanagement of money, and crooked transactions. We say that those who are dishonest, corrupt, unethical, and dishonorable shall not hold power in our country. We say that businesses that undermine the righteous and righteous causes shall lose their influence and fail to prosper. We speak that their dishonorable words, methods of communication, and intentions shall have no merit on the direction of the nation. We declare that the upright citizens and people of ethical principles and practices shall make way for and preserve our national prosperity. We say that all reasonable systems of checks and balances shall produce a high standard and shall be administered equally and fairly across the board. We say that the upright in word and deed shall lead the way for our states and cities so that they can flourish and succeed. We decree truth and integrity in business shall prevail, in Jesus' Name!

SCRIPTURE

Upright citizens are good for a city and make it prosper, but the talk of the wicked tears it apart (Proverbs 11:11 NLT).

WORD OF ENCOURAGEMENT

It's hard not to meet anyone these days who doesn't express their frustration with the countless areas across the country that have caused serious harm because of some form of lacking integrity or shady practices. Most are aware that government, big corporations, and countless private businesses have abused their power and misused resources for greed and gain on a wide scale. Common are the discussions on how our tax dollars are used to fund antibiblical causes, dangerous agendas, and activist or simply worthless programs. Worse, however, is that the average person feels nearly helpless to do anything to stop it. Of course, we cannot throw our hands in the air and abdicate our responsibility to make a difference where we are able. There are many ways the average person can get involved. In fact, there are more resources at our fingertips than ever to aid us in lifting our voice. When citizens begin to effect change on a grassroots level, amazing things happen! But we as Christians must be the leaders in effecting such change. We can't sit idly by and think it's not our "calling" to be involved in society's business structures, political systems, and public platforms. We cannot hide within the four walls of the church and hope our country will miraculously turn out right. The verse makes it clear that it's the involvement of the upright who make a city prosper. It's pointing to the righteous being involved in civil matters within our communities. We are to be an instrument of integrity that stands in the way of the crooked and unethical. Unless we become a halting force, evil will prevail. Let's begin taking our rightful place in enacting change, and let's also become the change by using our prayers to bring it to pass! Is anything too hard for God? No! He is well able to lift the standard of integrity in the business world when His people get involved and when they pray!

A LAND OF ADVANCEMENT AND INNOVATION

DECLARATION

We decree that our nation advances in its industrial innovation. We prophesy that this country is productive in manufacturing, building, infrastructure, and construction. We say that we are a nation of innovation in technology, business, and strategic growth. We say that those with new ideas, witty inventions, and creations shall arise and shall have motives to bless and do no harm. All scientific ideas and advances shall be used to help and shall not be used for evil intent. In Jesus' Name, we break the power of all demonic influences to build wicked inventions, merchandise, and harmful devices. We prophesy that medical breakthroughs shall be made available to undergird healing and well-being among the population. We declare God-breathed ideas shall blanket this nation and that God's people shall arise as innovators and lead the way in advancement. We say that the United States of America shall lead the way in all aspects of newly developed inventions and production.

We speak a divine surge in the advancement and innovation of our land! Amen!

SCRIPTURE

> *I wisdom dwell with prudence, and find out knowledge of witty inventions* (Proverbs 8:12 KJV).

> *Them hath he filled with wisdom of heart, to work all manner of work, of the engraver, and of the cunning workman, and of the embroiderer, in blue, and in purple, in scarlet, and in fine linen, and of the weaver, even of them that do any work, and of those that devise cunning work* (Exodus 35:35 KJV).

WORD OF ENCOURAGEMENT

It's obvious to those who trust in the Lord that the ability to create, invent, and build comes from God. We have creative ability because we are made in His image. When creative ideas and inventions are put into action, amazing things are the result. Nations that lead in advancement and innovations have influence and will reap prosperity.

Consider how the United States has led the way in many aspects of such advancement. It's been a key to our nation's heritage and is also an earmark of the Lord's blessings. Our technological advantage has clearly helped spread the Gospel worldwide and bless the nations of the earth.

When God instructed Moses to build the tabernacle in Exodus 35, it required skilled workers and those who had knowledge in certain crafts so that the end product was noteworthy. And notice that God instructed them to dress the tabernacle with the best materials too! This reveals that God knows the benefit of not only quality craftsmanship, but also the need for quality supplies. We may not realize how important it is to pray and decree along these lines as we pray for our country, but my question is, why don't we or why aren't we praying for it? It's a key component to the success of any nation and so it's important we include it in prayer. Let's begin a focused prayer effort and declare that not only will our nation be marked by creative ideas and productivity, but we will produce some of the most skilled workers, craftsmen, and inventors on planet Earth. Let's prophesy that the United States will lead the way in advancement and innovation!

Foreign Invasions Are Bound!

DECLARATION

We decree that all foreign invaders shall be cut off from the United States of America. We speak that all efforts to penetrate our borders shall fail. We prophesy that all terrorists, looters, meddlers, drug lords, gangsters, armies, squatters, and trespassers shall not be allowed entrance. We say that all foreign entities who would plot evil in our land shall be exposed, removed, and brought to justice, in Jesus' Name. We command all efforts to weaken the security and sovereignty of our nation to be bound and rendered ineffective. We declare all cyber invasions, tampering, and breaches shall be interrupted and stopped. We say that legislators and authorities shall pass laws that protect our borders and our cyber pathways from foreign interference, and they shall be dedicated to uphold such laws. We declare our borders, states, cities, and military institutions at home and abroad shall be protected and secured. We ask for angels to be released to stand watch and protect our land from all foreign entities that would invade it. We prophesy that foreign invasions are bound!

SCRIPTURE

> *The Lord will answer and say to His people, "Behold, I will send you grain and new wine and oil, and you will be satisfied by them; I will no longer make you a reproach among the nations. But I will remove far from you the northern army, and will drive him away into a barren and desolate land, with his face toward the eastern sea and his back toward the western sea; his stench will come up, and his foul odor will rise, because he has done monstrous things"* (Joel 2:19-20 NKJV).

WORD OF ENCOURAGEMENT

Countries are made of borders. Period. Every nation must have secure borders that keep out foreign invaders, whether those invaders be physical or virtual. Consider that God has borders. In the Old Testament He placed a border around Mt. Sinai when His presence descended, which no person was to cross. Heaven has a border and no one whose name isn't in the Lamb's Book of Life will enter. Borders and boundaries are healthy and necessary. Without them the result is chaos and confusion.

We have seen considerable effort by leaders, politicians, and the progressive left to break down our borders and leave them open and unsecure. This has wreaked havoc and is something we need to absolutely take hold of in prayer! As citizens, we must certainly be involved in asking our governing representatives and authorities to secure our borders, but we can also call upon Heaven. We can ask God to commission His angels to protect our borders. We can pray that those who would create cyber breaches will be exposed, and we can pray against military invasions and acts of terror. Often the most effective thing we can do regarding this matter is pray. Without prayer, we are left to the work of political figures, many of whom do not have our nation's best interests at heart. But remember, prayer and the declarations of the righteous can change things! We can decree that God will open the minds of our authorities to the importance of secure borders and that they will see the impact that unsecure borders will have. We can declare and all foreign invasions in our nation will be bound in Jesus' Name!

BENEFICIAL INTERNATIONAL ALLIANCES

DECLARATION

We decree that the United States of America shall make alliances with nations that shall undergird her sovereignty and biblical heritage. We speak that our president, leaders, and ambassadors shall only engage in treaties, agreements, accords, and coalitions with those who have our best interests at heart. We bind partnerships and affiliations developed through personal gain and greed, which undermine the prosperity, safety, and flourishing of our nation. We prophesy an exposure of all underhanded dealings, dishonest exchanges, and deceitful schemes, in Jesus' Name. We declare the demonic influence to tie this country to nations and governments who seek to destroy our stability and demean our godly principles shall be broken by the power of God. We command a breaking of alliances and agreements currently placed that are imposing harm upon our country. In their stead, we prophesy that alliances shall be established for the good of all citizens, which will provide stability and peace to future generations. We speak transparency and accountability to the arm of foreign affairs, and we decree that all meetings, discussions, and conventions shall produce beneficial results. We speak that all alliances shall be beneficial, in Jesus' Name!

SCRIPTURE

> *You shall make no covenant with them or with their gods. They shall not live in your land, otherwise they will make you sin against Me; for if you serve their gods, it is certain to be a snare to you* (Exodus 23:32-33 NASB).

WORD OF ENCOURAGEMENT

Most of us can recall some kind of event in our nation's foreign affairs that has been utterly egregious. Our minds go to some of the most evil agreements, poor decisions made militarily, and the like. Many have resulted in unnecessary deaths of the innocent and painful experiences by those who had no choice in the matter. More infuriating is government officials who do not seem to care about the people and only have their own personal interests at heart. It seems secular government is increasingly committed to making alliances with foreign leaders who are entirely disconnected from the biblical foundation of our country and are actually our enemies altogether. It can at times feel hopeless, except that our hope is in the living God who has preserved and kept us!

As God's people, we should pray and decree over the foreign affairs of the nation. We can call upon Heaven to invade the state department and cause a divine alignment with that which will protect and bring peace. We can intervene by asking the Lord to hover over our defense department so that military actions will be carried out for the right reasons and in the right way and timing. We must also have faith that God is in control. It's important that we don't just jump on the wagon of complaints whenever we hear something negative along these lines in the news. We need to be the bulwark that will stand between Heaven and earth in intercession to bring the foolishness of man under subjection to God's purposes. When you witness the negative, it's not the time to give up hope but the time to use our authority in the spirit and prophesy that our leaders will make beneficial international alliances and decisions in Jesus' Name!

PROTECTION FOR EMERGENCY RESPONDERS

DECLARATION

We decree that the emergency and first responders in our nation shall be protected and preserved. We prophesy that they shall be safe as they tend to dangerous and unstable situations. We prophesy an anointing of preservation to be upon every firefighter, police officer, medical professional, and paramedic. We prophesy protection over the professionals involved in all aspects of emergency rescue, search, and recovery. We declare they shall perform their duties efficiently and with physical and emotional strength. We bind the spirit of accident, tragedy, death, and calamity from harming them in Jesus' Name! We take authority over all post-traumatic stress, and we declare it cannot bind itself to their soul. May the hardships and difficulties they encounter on the field not draw them into depression or despondency. We prophesy the Lord's peace to be upon them and their families. We declare whenever they leave their homes for work, they shall return safely. We bind the attempts of the attacker, lawless and rebellious, from imposing harm upon law enforcement and security personnel. We pray that every first responder will uphold their position with expertise and professionalism and will receive appreciation and value from the public. We say that the Lord's supernatural hand and His mighty angels shall place a guard of protection upon every first and emergency responder in the United States of America!

SCRIPTURE

The Lord shall preserve thy going out and thy coming in from this time forth, and even for evermore (Psalm 121:8 KJV).

WORD OF ENCOURAGEMENT

Every tragic event we have ever seen in the news serves to highlight the work of first and emergency responders. If not for their willingness to fly in the face of danger, countless tragic situations may have turned for the worse. Unless we have been in their field of work, we cannot possibly grasp all the challenges they deal with each day in such a high adrenaline environment. It's why the demand to "defund the police" is so grievous. We know that our law enforcement professionals do so much more for the community than enforce the law. They are also first responders on some of the most tragic accidents and rescues, many of which include infants and children. If not for all our emergency responders, life as we know it would be so much different and the stability we have as a nation would be gone. They need to know that society supports them and is appreciative of their years of hard training and dedication to the betterment and well-being of all citizens.

Undoubtedly, one of the ways we can change America is to pray for our first responders and ask God to protect them. They need our prayers of strength and support, and whenever we encounter or meet one we need to let them know we pray for them and value them! Our prayers and decrees of faith will move God's hand and the commissioning of Heaven's angels to surround and preserve them.

CRIME AND VIOLENCE BROKEN

DECLARATION

We decree that the spirit of crime, lawlessness, and violence is broken upon our land. We prophesy that every demonic spirit that is promoting criminal activity, violent outbursts, civil disorder, and terrorism is bound in Jesus' Name. We declare that all who would intend to carry out shootings, robberies, gang violence, riots, rapes, murders, and human trafficking shall be disrupted and unable to commit such crimes. We prophesy that criminals who commit acts of misconduct, misdemeanors, and felonies shall be caught and brought to justice. We say that lawmakers, justices, and government officials shall defend the lawful and hold criminals accountable for their actions. We declare that the hearts of the criminally minded shall soften, change, and receive salvation. We decree they shall turn from their wickedness and repent of their sins. We speak a divine restraint from the Lord Himself comes upon them and prevents them from committing evil against the innocent. We say that our nation is a nation of lawfulness, virtue, obedience, and order. We decree crime and violence are broken in Jesus' Name!

SCRIPTURE

Violence shall no more be heard in thy land, wasting nor destruction within thy borders; but thou shalt call thy walls Salvation, and thy gates Praise (Isaiah 60:18 KJV).

WORD OF ENCOURAGEMENT

Jesus said that in the last days people's hearts will grow harder and lawlessness would increase (see Matt. 24:12). The apostle Paul further said that these times would be marked by the ill-behaved (see 2 Tim. 3:1-8). Yet in both accounts they each offer a word of hope. Jesus said we must see to it that our hearts are not troubled (see Matt. 24:6), and then be reminded that in this very environment the good news of the Gospel would go forth (see Matt. 24:14)! Paul then said the folly of the sinfully minded would be made manifest for all to see and their wicked actions will be interrupted (see 2 Tim. 3:9).

The summary is that in times when criminal acts seem to be mounting the Gospel will impact the culture, and there will be good news! This means even the criminally minded and their intended actions can be supernaturally interrupted by the power of God!

This is why we can decree and prophesy that statistics of crimes across this nation can be on the decline, *not* increasing! Just because it's the end times does not mean we stop binding the works of the devil in prayer. We must command the demons that are driving the lawlessness in our communities to be bound. We need to call for the angels to bring safety and security and ask the Lord to change the hearts and minds of evildoers before they can carry out such acts. We also need to pray for those in the justice system that they will be motivated to ensure that criminals are brought to justice and that the innocent will be defended and protected. Your decree today commanding crime and violence to be bound will affect our nation and prevent evil from prevailing! We decree crime and violence are broken over America!

DECLARATION

We decree a release of angelic activity over our nation! As the people of God, the angels are servants sent forth from Heaven to work on our behalf, and therefore we release them on assignment for this nation. We call upon Heaven for a commissioning of the hosts to go forth and cover the United States of America and keep it from evil. We stand in confident assurance because of the work of angelic forces all around us. They are standing against the principalities, powers, against the rulers of the darkness of this world, and spiritual wickedness in high places. The angels are obstructing the work of the destroyer and they are making this nation safe. The angels shall keep us from all manner of destruction and terror. We call for the angels to wage war in the gates over Washington, DC, and drive out the demonic strongholds from our White House, Capitol, Supreme Court, Pentagon, and from all historical sites and monuments. We say the angels are warring in the seats of government all across this land. We call for the angelic armies to protect this nation from the effects of war and international conflict. Let the angels be posted in all key areas, in every state, region, and city, and we prophesy, "Let the angels of God be released in the United States of America!"

SCRIPTURE

Therefore, angels are only servants—spirits sent to care for people who will inherit salvation (Hebrews 1:14 NLT).

Bless the Lord, ye his angels, that excel in strength, that do his commandments, hearkening unto the voice of his word (Psalm 103:20 KJV).

WORD OF ENCOURAGEMENT

If we as believers truly understood that Heaven's angels are here on assignment for us, it might change our outlook in many areas. And if angels *are* ministering servants specifically for us, then they are here on assignment for everything that affects us. Therefore, we can safely presume that they are working on assignment in our nation, since what happens in our country affects us all. Sometimes looking at the evil of the day, we can forget this powerful fact! If we get focused on all the negative that is happening or what the news media reports, we will overlook the operations of angels around us. We may fail to see how much they are interrupting the enemy's agenda and holding back the flood of darkness.

We know the true war behind everything we see is spiritual. Ephesians 6:12 makes it clear that our battle is not with flesh and blood. Of course, we will have to interact with flesh and blood in that conflict, but the Bible is reminding us here to keep our eyes on the war behind the war. There is no doubt that unseen demonic powers are hovering over our nation's capital in an effort to enact their agenda. Yet we must know God's angels are there to counter them! We have the power as the saints of God to call for Heaven's angels to not only watch us personally but insert themselves in the spiritual battle over this nation! Let Heaven's hosts be released!

NO FAKE NEWS!

DECLARATION

We decree that the United States of America shall have news and media outlets that shall report the truth. They shall report news correctly and accurately without any omitting of facts and without spinning stories. We declare a defunding of media outlets and publications that use propaganda for evil agendas and antichrist views. We say they shall be exposed in their lies and misrepresentation of the facts. We decree fake news shall lose its influence across the nation and will no longer be able to avoid truthful reporting. We prophesy that the covers are torn back so that they shall have no choice but to acknowledge accurate data, details, and information. We declare news channels and publications shall be raised up that shall report and print articles that are in support of conservative, moral, and biblical values. We speak prosperity and success to the honest and truthful outlets and say that they shall gain national and international support. We declare, let truth prevail in the media, and there shall be a commitment by executives, journalists, anchors, and reporters to gather and communicate the truth. We declare fake news shall not control this nation, in Jesus' Name!

SCRIPTURE

Thou shalt not raise a false report: put not thine hand with the wicked to be an unrighteous witness (Exodus 23:1 KJV).

WORD OF ENCOURAGEMENT

We would all be extremely thrilled if we were confident that the stories we hear on the news or in magazines and across social media pages were not only accurate, but truthful. Imagine how the nation might be different if news agencies actually reported the facts as they happen and didn't cherry-pick stories that support a certain agenda. Consider the benefit if those same agencies actually reported important stories rather than silly gossip columns that are simply a waste of time and money. We have all also witnessed the damage caused by the mainstream media when they unite to destroy anything against their narratives. Is it even possible to see news outlets emerge that are dedicated to honest and noteworthy reports? Yes, and some have arisen, and we thank God for that, but we can also agree that there needs to be a shift in the mainstream that supports the values most decent Americans and Christians hold dear.

I believe this *can* and is shifting! Sure, it may not all be an immediate thing, but if we pray for it so much can change. We need to ask ourselves whether we have truly sought Heaven over the matter. Also, what are we speaking regarding it? We are probably all guilty of complaining about the fake propaganda that dominates most of the airways. And of course, we definitely should call out these false reports and reporters, but we also need to pray and ask God to raise up quality news outlets that are honest, truthful, and committed to reporting noteworthy news. Many such outlets *are* rising, and we need to support them, pray for their success, and decree that false reports and narratives will no longer be able to dominate this nation! Let's decree no fake news in America!

We the People *of the United States, in order to form a more perfect Union, establish Justice, insure domestic Tranquility, provide for the common defence, promote the general Welfare, and secure the Blessings of Liberty to ourselves and our Posterity, do ordain and establish this Constitution for the United States of America.*

Article I *Article II*

EVIL INFLUENCERS DEFUNDED

DECLARATION

We decree that every person, business, corporation, and government entity that would influence this nation with evil will lose money and their efforts shall be defunded. We prophesy that every individual and group that would give financial support to wicked causes will not prosper, and their efforts shall be defeated, in Jesus' Name. We break the power and plans of those who make shady deals, launder money, and use their money for evil. We declare that all influencers who trade money with foreign entities for evil and criminal purposes shall be exposed and brought to justice. We decree that all financial exchanges, both domestic and international, that would harm this nation shall be disrupted. We say that those in our government who have a wicked agenda to promote or fund causes that further perversion, sexualize the culture, and promote violence and tension shall be removed from their offices and have no more power to supply money for such efforts. We declare all sources of money exchanged by greed, criminal activities, drugs, human trafficking, black market operations, or to sell perverse products shall become bankrupt. We speak bankruptcy to the wicked and prosperity to the righteous, and we say that all evil influencers within and outside the United States of America who want to bring harm to this country shall go financially broke, in Jesus' Name!

SCRIPTURE

In the house of the righteous is much treasure: but in the revenues of the wicked is trouble (Proverbs 15:6 KJV).

WORD OF ENCOURAGEMENT

Money in and of itself isn't evil, but it can bring out either the worst or best in people. First Timothy 6:10 is often misquoted as money being the root of all evil, but it actually says the *love* of money is the root of all evil. This means when a person loves money over God, eventually they will let go of their good character and proper priorities to obtain money. This is what we commonly see with those who have evil intent. They will do anything and everything for money, including committing criminal acts if they feel it's in their interests to do so. All too many are the incidences of some individual, group, or government entity mishandling money to further evil agendas.

For the righteous, money is simply a resource to accomplish good, spread the Gospel, and influence society with righteousness. Money in the wrong hands influences the culture with darkness, but money in the right hands can shift it toward righteousness. We need to pray that those who have money and are using it for evil purposes will go bankrupt and that their deep pockets are suddenly filled with holes. For this nation to be shifted toward righteousness we need individuals, businesses, and government entities who will use their resources to further righteous causes. It's time for money to be in the right hands so this nation will prosper and be blessed by God. It's also time for all evil influencers to lose money and be defunded in Jesus' Name!

JOBS AND BUSINESSES EXCEL

DECLARATION

We decree that the jobs and businesses in this nation shall excel and succeed. We declare a national increase in new jobs, business ventures, employment, trade skills, and achieved career paths. We break the power of joblessness, unemployment, bankruptcy, and business failure. We bind the spirit of poverty from ruling in our country. We come against the trends toward inflation and command it to stabilize in Jesus' Name. We prophesy that capitalism, free enterprise, and industrialism shall explode with progress. We speak to the honorable small businesses of our nation and command them to survive and expand! We prophesy to their financial bottom line and say, "Grow, in Jesus' Name!" We decree that these businesses shall be able to attain their goals and their bank accounts shall be full. We say that through their business more job positions shall be made available. We declare that those who are jobless will find gainful and stable employment. We declare that all Christian and faith-based businesses shall overflow with wealth, and we say that the United States of America shall be marked by ongoing job growth and businesses shall excel in our land!

SCRIPTURE

> *But thou shalt remember the Lord thy God: for it is he that giveth thee power to get wealth, that he may establish his covenant which he sware unto thy fathers, as it is this day* (Deuteronomy 8:18 KJV).

WORD OF ENCOURAGEMENT

Job growth is the sign of a healthy economy; and the ability to find work that is fulfilling and gainful, fulfills a key component in the human heart. It causes us to strive and experience the benefit of personal development. God designed us to work, and He wants us to excel at what we do! He created Adam and Eve and placed them in the Garden of Eden to till and keep it. There is something about working at a craft and being employed to make money that satisfies a God-given desire for accomplishment. It's part of our nature that thirsts for a creative outlet and to have a stable existence on earth.

However, often poorly managed governments are the culprit behind a collective decline in jobs. Things like out-of-control inflation, high taxes, and so on cause many businesses to operate at a minimum or close their doors altogether. This is something we must decree against! This is even more important during times when those with evil intent are behaving foolishly and, in some cases, actually seeking out ways to destroy the job market. Yet we as God's people have the authority to interrupt it though prayer, and we have the faith to see their plans disrupted by Heaven's intervention. Let's pray for businesses and job growth and believe that every business that operates with integrity will prosper!

HEALING FROM RACIAL TENSIONS

We decree that racial divisions, tensions, and misunderstandings all across our nation are healed. We say that any hostility and bitterness is overtaken by kindness and goodwill. We break the power of accusation, suspicion, biases, and misconceptions, in Jesus' Name. We declare a supernatural love, appreciation, and understanding arises between cultures, races, and creeds. We prophesy that all those who would seek to stir unjustified racial wars, race baiting, and prejudiced ideologies shall not be given a voice or platform. We bind the power of all racially motivated activists and extremists from misconstruing racial issues in the United States of America. We declare that racially motivated violence and protests shall be replaced by love, forgiveness, dialogue, and communication. We bind false narratives and ideologies about race, and we declare they are replaced by truthfulness and accuracy. We ask the Holy Spirit of Truth to be released upon the citizens of this nation to see other races as God sees them. We declare an understanding that all people are of one blood, created in the image of God, and are of precious value. We say leaders and influencers who promote unity among the races shall arise and that this nation shall experience unprecedented racial wholeness in Jesus' Name!

SCRIPTURE

> *And hath made of one blood all nations of men for to dwell on all the face of the earth, and hath determined the times before appointed, and the bounds of their habitation* (Acts 17:26 KJV).

WORD OF ENCOURAGEMENT

Racism is real. There is no question about that, and it has existed for as long as time itself. Its ugliness has resulted in some of the worst tragedies in history, including the infamous Holocaust. Racism is nothing short of demonic, and this country, like many countries, has had its own challenges against this evil. However, in the middle of that there are always those who look to stir the pot of racism and create divisions even in situations where they don't exist. The United States has been known as the great melting pot welcoming all races, yet there are some who are committed to turn this country into the great boiling pot. They manipulate historical accounts and current incidences of racism to further their destructive ideology that our country is inherently racist. This extreme viewpoint only muddies the waters for any attempts to bring racial wholeness. Truth is, most average, freedom-loving Americans are far from racist. They may not always understand one another's cultures, but they aren't racist. Bona fide racism is not as widespread in this country as some are determined to solicit. Good citizens of all backgrounds want nothing more than to join hands with their brothers and sisters of a different race. Yet so often this element gets ignored. It's time for us as Christians to begin heralding the mass unity among races that already exists and show the world that we love one another. Let's bind in prayer the demonic powers of racism and loose the love of God, unity, and healing. Let's be the catalyst for racial healing in our nation!

We the People *of the United States, in order to form a more perfect Union, establish Justice,
insure domestic Tranquility, provide for the common defence, promote the general Welfare, and secure the Blessings of Liberty to ourselves
and our Posterity, do ordain and establish this Constitution for the United States of America.*

PEACE UPON THE WEATHER

DECLARATION

We decree over the weather in the United States and we say that it is consistent and calm. This nation shall not be marked by excessive turbulent weather patterns. We declare a divine protection from the power of severe storms, tornadoes, blizzards, earthquakes, hurricanes, volcanic eruptions, drought, and flooding. We rebuke extreme heat, cold, and wind, in Jesus' Name. We bind demonic activity from manipulating the weather in this nation. We prophesy that there shall not be mass destruction, accidents, injuries, and death because of violent and unstable weather. We prophesy stability to the weather across our nation and may it be marked by moderate atmospheric conditions. May there be gentle and beneficial rains, clear skies, comfortable temperatures, and moisture. We say all industries affected by weather shall experience fruitful seasons of growth. We prophesy that the farmers of this nation shall experience seasons of good weather. May the Lord shine upon this land and cause the sun to rise upon the just and unjust that all may experience tranquility. We declare peace to the weather in the United States of America!

SCRIPTURE

> *And he arose, and rebuked the wind, and said unto the sea, Peace, be still. And the wind ceased, and there was a great calm* (Mark 4:39 KJV).

WORD OF ENCOURAGEMENT

We can often pass serious weather patterns off as a normal occurrence and, yes, in the broad sense of it they are. However, we also know that satan, who is also referred to as the prince of the power of the air (see Eph. 2:2), inserts himself in tragic weather. We see this in Mark 4:35-41, when Jesus and His disciples crossed the sea and a storm arose. Jesus rebuked the storm and it immediately calmed. That deadly storm certainly wasn't from God or Jesus wouldn't have countered it and commanded it to cease. Immediately after Jesus and His disciples came to the shore they met the demoniac of Gadara who had been tormenting that entire area. It's very clear there was a demonic entity involved in the storm attempting to resist Jesus and disrupt His agenda to free the demon-possessed man.

It only stands to reason that deadly and destructive storms are influenced by demon spirits. We can counter their forces and ask God to calm the weather. Like Jesus, we can decree, "Peace, be still!" In fact, in the story in Mark 4, Jesus had expected His disciples to use their own faith regarding the weather. He asked them, "Where is your faith?" It would seem that Jesus was intentional on being asleep to give the disciples an opportunity to use the faith and the power He had given them against evil forces. Let's use our faith and spiritual authority to declare peace upon the weather over our nation!

GOVERNMENTAL ABUSES
OF POWER RESTRAINED

DECLARATION

We decree that those in seats and offices of government who misuse and abuse their power shall be restrained. We prophesy that elected officials, attorneys, judges, lawmakers, tax agencies, corporations, institutions, and all organizations shall be limited to the fair application of the law, and that such law will be applied equally for all. They shall not find ways to abuse their power for personal gain or interests. They will not indict and sentence the innocent to advance an unrighteous purpose. We bind the demonic influence driving governmental abuses of authority in the Name of Jesus! We say that all falsely calculated efforts by high-level leaders, designed to harm their opponents or constituents, shall be exposed as fraudulent and struck down as absurd. We bind the work of liars who spread unjust defamation, and we say they shall be held accountable. We declare that God will raise up fair and righteous leadership all across our nation, and the citizens of this nation shall welcome their good works. We decree legislation will be passed on a federal and state level to promote and bring about true justice, which shall expose misrepresentation. We decree governmental abuse and misuse shall be restrained, in Jesus' Name!

SCRIPTURE

Don't be surprised if you see a poor person being oppressed by the powerful and if justice is being miscarried throughout the land. For every official is under orders from higher up, and matters of justice get lost in red tape and bureaucracy (Ecclesiastes 5:8 NLT).

Arise, O Lord; let not man prevail: let the heathen be judged in thy sight. Put them in fear, O Lord: that the nations may know themselves to be but men. Selah (Psalm 9:19-20 KJV).

WORD OF ENCOURAGEMENT

Imagine a nation where governmental abuses are limited and held to account. It seems extreme to say the least! We use the term Deep State to speak of those individuals and groups of governmental authorities who target their adversaries through legal misuses and abuses while they find a way to wiggle free from any legal accountability. We have seen a great deal of this not only in our nation, but nations around the world for centuries.

Looking at our Scriptures, we can find assurance in the fact that governmental abuse of power is nothing new. It happened throughout Scripture, it happened throughout history, and it's happened in our nation long before most of us can remember. Yet the Bible shows us countless examples where abusive leaders were ultimately restrained by God and eventually removed, harshly in many cases. Make no mistake that God holds all dishonest leaders accountable for their sinful lifestyles and abusive ways. The Bible is clear throughout that the wicked will have their day of justice. In the meantime, as God determines these outcomes, we can pray that the demonic agenda behind such leaders will be restrained and unable to operate!

WITCHCRAFT AND CURSES BROKEN

DECLARATION

We decree the power and activity of witchcraft and the occult that is working against this nation is bound and rendered powerless in the Name of Jesus! We break the power of every curse, spell, incantation, and hex spoken by the workers of divination. We declare that all words uttered using sorcery to sabotage the United States of America shall fall to the ground and have no effect. We bind the release of demons authorized by occultic practices and rituals. We say that the workers of witchcraft and magic shall lose their ability to alter the blessing of this country and all demonic control crumbles and falls. We prophesy that the groups, clubs, gatherings, covens, and assemblies of satanic worship shall be dissolved. We say that all their monuments and symbols of idolatry and satanism shall be torn down and removed! We condemn and reverse every curse already in motion and command it to return to the place from which it was sent. We decree that the curse is null and void and we say it is replaced with blessing and peace. We loose angelic activity to war against demons in the heavenlies and to bring about an outpouring of God's goodness and covering to this land. We stand firm and decree that all witchcraft curses in this nation are removed and entirely broken in Jesus' Name!

SCRIPTURE

And I will give unto thee the keys of the kingdom of Heaven: and whatsoever thou shalt bind on earth shall be bound in Heaven: and whatsoever thou shalt loose on earth shall be loosed in Heaven (Matthew 16:19 KJV).

WORD OF ENCOURAGEMENT

We always have to remind ourselves of what goes on in the unseen spiritual world that we can't physically see. As believers, we must stay aware of the war behind the scenes. We can't neglect the legitimacy of the occult and its effect on a nation. Here in the United States and in much of the Western world, witchcraft and sorcery are often presented and accepted as little more than fun and fantasy. Many people have little comprehension that there are serious occult groups who are dedicated to unleashing the demonic in every sector of society. What many think is hocus-pocus or magic games, members of the occult are taking it seriously and using witchcraft for all manner of evil. They are committed to the regular practice of satanic rituals, supernatural experiences through demonic power, and the like, and their endgame is to have absolute control over the nation.

As believers, the Bible is clear that we have authority against the devil and his minions. What we bind on earth is bound in the heavens. Through our faith-filled words and the power of Jesus' Name, we can interrupt and break the communications and transmissions that the workers of divination are releasing against our country. We can also bind these demons from influencing society into a moral decline and general acceptance of corruption. Our declaration over our great nation is that the work of witchcraft and all curses are bound in the Name of Jesus!

THE NAME OF JESUS GLORIFIED

DECLARATION

We decree that the Name of Jesus shall be exalted and lifted high over this nation! We say that His Name shall be exonerated and declared in public places, buildings, courtrooms, and businesses. We prophesy that the Name of Jesus shall be welcomed in our schools, sporting events, political places, upon television screens, and in the media. We say that His Name shall be honored and not used to curse. We break the power of all demonic entities from dishonoring Jesus' Name, and may the mouths of those who would take the Name of the Lord in vain be silenced. We declare that no atheists or heathenistic organizations shall succeed in their attempt to remove the honor of Jesus' Name from the public square. We prophesy that the knee of the resistant, hard-hearted, and sinner shall bow to Jesus' Name. We decree that their tongues shall acknowledge and confess His lordship. The Name of Jesus shall be exalted by the president, vice president, and the presidential cabinet. We say His Name shall be exalted by the Congress, the Supreme Court, by all branches of our government, and by the military. We declare that prayer and public addresses shall be presented in the Name of Jesus Christ. We release an awakening to the honor of His matchless Name in society, and we prophesy that the Name of Jesus shall stand glorified above every other name in our nation!

SCRIPTURE

Wherefore God also hath highly exalted him, and given him a name which is above every name: that at the Name of Jesus every knee should bow, of things in Heaven, and things in earth, and things under the earth; and that every tongue should confess that Jesus Christ is Lord, to the glory of God the Father (Philippians 2:9-11 KJV).

Be still, and know that I am God: I will be exalted among the heathen, I will be exalted in the earth (Psalm 46:10 KJV).

WORD OF ENCOURAGEMENT

The Bible is clear: when the Name of Jesus is lifted up, men will be drawn to Him (see John 12:32)! America is a nation that was built upon Christian principles, and the intent of our early forefathers was to allow citizens to exalt Jesus' Name and worship Him without restriction. We should not be ashamed by the fact that this country was built upon a Christian foundation, nor should we be intimidated by critics who want to erase that heritage and history. We need to take a confident stand to keep the Name of Jesus from being removed from our public places and from our political arenas. We need to lead the way in confessing the Name of Jesus Christ before men when it's not popular and when there is opposition against it. Of late, we have seen the attempts by atheistic groups who want to stamp out all mention of Jesus Christ and Christian values. We cannot allow it, and our prayer and declaration must be that the Name of the Lord Jesus will be honored and revered all across this great land. Sure, one day every knee will bow down and confess Jesus is Lord, but we can also expect that to happen now so that we can truly call the United States a nation where the Name of Jesus is glorified!

SICKNESS, PLAGUES, AND DISEASES REMOVED

DECLARATION

We decree the powers of disease, sickness, illness, and plagues are removed from our nation. We call upon the Lord God to take away the environment of disease from the people, and we say that this nation shall not be marked by infirmity. We command every outbreak, malady, and invasion of disease to be neutralized by the hand of God! In Jesus' Name, we declare that the pharmaceutical industry, medical centers, research institutions, the Center for Disease Control, and World Health Organization cannot restrict medical breakthroughs or healing remedies for financial gain or any other agenda. We decree they cannot inflict the populace with harm through gain of function research, intentionally released epidemics and viruses, or through the poisoning of food, water, and medicines. We break the power of any entities from controlling the public through the means of falsified measures and mandates regarding health and wellness. We prophesy a manifested wave of healing, health, and wholeness to blanket this land. We call upon the Lord to remove sickness far from us, and we call America a nation of health, wellness, and wholeness in Jesus' Name!

SCRIPTURE

And the Lord will take away from thee all sickness, and will put none of the evil diseases of Egypt, which thou knowest, upon thee; but will lay them upon all them that hate thee (Deuteronomy 7:15 KJV).

WORD OF ENCOURAGEMENT

God has always made a provision of healing for His people. He told Israel that if they would serve Him, He would promise to remove sickness from their midst. Scriptures promising divine health are woven throughout the Bible, which reveals God's heart for people to live in good health and wholeness. Of course, people's poor choices can open them to various illnesses, but the key is to know God's intent is for people to be well.

That said, one might ask if we can really ask God to supply healing power for an entire nation. While He did that for Israel, His chosen people, does that truly apply to other nations? First, we must realize that we, the Church, are also His chosen people. As His people, we can ask God to heal our nation and cause it the be marked by healing rather than be invaded by widespread disease. While it seems the pandemic of 2020 caught many believers off guard, imagine what might have happened if Christians across our nation began to pray and decree against the disease rather than recoil in fear. I believe the pandemic taught us many things that we need to improve and do better, one being we need to stand up in the anointing against the power of sickness. If we can pray for our nation regarding countless other things, why can't we pray and ask God to heal our nation, not just spiritually, but physically? Why can't we pray and ask God for a wave of healing to blanket our land? We definitely need to do this and declare in faith that sickness, plagues, and disease shall not invade our land in Jesus' Name!

WICKED LEGISLATIONS DISRUPTED

DECLARATION

We decree that our nation shall be marked by righteous laws and legislation. We declare that new bills shall not be embedded with covert measures that further immorality and wickedness. Bills intended to subvert our nation's sovereignty or the Constitution shall be divinely disrupted. We say that all such attempts will be exposed and thrown out. In the Name of Jesus, we bind the demonic craftiness of those who work to devise evil laws. We declare that they shall not be able to execute their plans. We prophesy that both state and federal house legislators shall be driven toward moral law and shall be committed to enacting such laws. We say they shall uphold laws that defend life, liberty, and the pursuit of happiness. They will pass laws that reduce the excess tax burden on the people of our nation. They will defend bills and legislation that liberate the Lord's Church from restrictions. We prophesy that legislation and laws for the good of the people will become the norm, and legislation that furthers moral decline shall not even be considered. We declare this nation is a nation of upright and moral law, and all attempts to create wicked legislations are interrupted and disrupted in Jesus' Name!

SCRIPTURE

It is an abomination to kings to commit wickedness: for the throne is established by righteousness (Proverbs 16:12 KJV).

WORD OF ENCOURAGEMENT

Laws are intended to create social order and place boundaries on people to prevent misconduct and crime. They also are designed to eliminate excesses that impose extreme demands on the public. More recently, we have witnessed an increasing number of bills being presented, and in some cases passed, that are unreasonable in nature. They are designed to benefit a small group of extremists while threatening the acceptable well-being of the larger population. In many cases, such excessive pieces of legislation are endangering innocent children, to which we cannot turn a blind eye. We must also realize that many lawmakers who are bent upon such unreasonable legislation purposefully try to hide these excesses by embedding them in other seemingly beneficial bills. A large part of the population is often left unaware of the specific bills where this is happening, and therefore find it difficult to be involved in interrupting them.

This is where prayer becomes so important. Through our decrees of faith, we can serve notice to the demonic operations behind such things and disrupt them even when they are creatively hidden from public view. We can also call upon Heaven to expose these acts and raise up the right lawmakers who are committed to drafting bills that are decent in nature. We can also pray that these bills that are truly beneficial will pass and become law while immoral and wicked law is disrupted in Jesus' Name!

We the People of the United States, in order to form a more perfect Union, establish Justice, insure domestic Tranquility, provide for the common defence, promote the general Welfare, and secure the Blessings of Liberty to ourselves and our Posterity, do ordain and establish this Constitution for the United States of America.

Article I   Article II

BOLD BELIEVERS ARISING

DECLARATION

We decree that the company of believers across this nation shall be filled with a heavenly and holy boldness. We declare that the Church of the Lord Jesus Christ shall stand confident in her message without wavering. We prophesy that God's people shall stand in positions of influence and not cower or be intimidated by those who carry an antichrist spirit. We break a spirit of cowardice, fearfulness, and faintheartedness, in Jesus' Name. We declare that believers everywhere shall courageously arise and insert themselves in the key issues of society and be a voice of moral righteousness and truth. We pray for Christians to impact the culture with biblical values and boldly defend the Christian heritage of the United States of America. We declare the pulpits of our nation shall be filled with pastors and leaders who are fearless and unafraid to address all realms of society and public life in accordance with the Bible. We say that bold believers shall arise in our government, schools, churches, workforce, and media. They shall speak the truth without wavering regarding every issue that goes against the Word of God. We prophesy that pastors, leaders, and believers shall rightly teach the Scriptures and not shy away from passages deemed offensive by the culture. We say that bold believers are arising in America, in Jesus' Name!

SCRIPTURE

The wicked flee when no man pursueth: but the righteous are bold as a lion (Proverbs 28:1 KJV).

And now, Lord, behold their threatenings: and grant unto thy servants, that with all boldness they may speak thy word (Acts 4:29 KJV).

WORD OF ENCOURAGEMENT

The trait that marked the early apostles of the Book of Acts was that they were exceptionally bold. In Acts 4, they were threatened, beaten, and jailed by the governmental authorities and religious establishment for preaching about Jesus in the public square. Rather than be intimidated or given to fear, they prayed that God would give them an even greater measure of boldness! It was almost as if they felt their current level of boldness wasn't sufficient!

Today, many American Christians live to simply "play nice" with the culture. They are fearful of ending up in the crosshairs of criticism and persecution. They don't want to be involved in the places of government where ideologies and laws are being advanced that aim to destroy our Christian heritage. They think the only area where they should go beyond the four walls of the church is for the purpose of humanitarian outreach. And while that is a key role of the church, the same church should also insert itself in the moral compass of our culture. Believers need to stand up for truth in our school systems, workplaces, and governmental arenas. Christians also need to become a countering force against the lies of the media. Unless we arise, our Christian influence in these sectors of society will only continue to erode, eventually leaving our nation to become a fully secularized society. Without our bold voice, where is the world going to hear the truth? We need bold believers to arise!

GOD'S MERCY AND HELP UPON US

DECLARATION

We decree that the United States of America shall receive the mercy of the Lord and forgiveness for her sins. We ask that God's grace and merciful kindness be extended to our land and that He will help us! We declare that all demonic operations that would draw our nation into judgment and affliction are bound in Jesus' Name. We say, let the teeth of the wicked be shattered and unable to advance the curse upon our land. We say every effort to release sin, immorality, and iniquity shall fail and it will not open this nation to calamity. We call for God's goodness to blanket our nation, allowing it to be marked with blessing, benevolence, and Heaven's generosity. We pray that the compassions of the Lord would remain upon the United States, and we would find merciful kindness from above. We declare this is a nation that calls upon the help of the Lord and asks for His guidance, involvement, and gracious favor. We decree that governmental leaders shall see the need for the Lord's mercy to rest upon us, and they shall acknowledge that His mercy and help is our only hope. We humbly cry out for the Lord's mercy, and we decree, may His supernatural help and provision be upon us in Jesus' Name!

SCRIPTURE

It is of the Lord's mercies that we are not consumed, because his compassions fail not (Lamentations 3:22 KJV).

WORD OF ENCOURAGEMENT

The mercy of the Lord being extended to a nation truly is its only hope. As our Scripture verse above shows, if not for His mercy we would all be consumed. It makes us realize just how much God's mercy has been upon the United States over the years. First, we are still here, and second, for the most part this nation has been very blessed. Many believers are quick to say America is being judged anytime something bad happens or because of the grievous sin in parts of the culture. However, sometimes we also fail to recognize how many in society are still pursuing God, praying, and asking for the Lord's involvement.

Undoubtedly, the Lord's mercy is being extended because of it. We can't forget how much good has covered this land, particularly in comparison to other nations of the world. Our prayer needs to be that governmental leaders in all areas will look to God and know that without His mercy we are doomed. Perhaps it's the reason our dollar bills still say, "In God we trust." It's because deep in their heart, most Americans know that we need God. They may not want to acknowledge that consciously, but deep down they know this nation needs God and so they aren't quick to fully remove Him.

Right now, we need believers who haven't given up on America and aren't willing to turn it over to judgment just because of those who are bent upon evil. We need to continually cry out for God's mercy and help! God can and will extend mercy for those who ask, and our cry is certainly more powerful than the actions of evildoers. We need to stand in faith that God's mercy and help will remain upon the United States of America!

EDUCATIONAL REFORMATION

DECLARATION

We decree that the education systems of this nation experience a reform. We prophesy that the school and university boards turn toward a righteous and proper educational agenda. We declare that curricula and classes shall be for the purpose of quality education, not evil indoctrination. In the Name of Jesus, we break the power of all demonically inspired programs, subjects, syllabuses, and courses that teach antibiblical and improper content. We decree that books, periodicals, online information, and papers that contain immoral and anti-American messages shall be removed from the classrooms and libraries. We decree every educator, teacher, and professor determined to instill indecent, antichrist, leftist, and socialist subject matter shall be removed. We declare a pushback arises against federal, state, and local school boards who advance offensive material and who prevent parents from being informed regarding their child's education. We say that parents shall be given full access to their child's curriculum and shall have the right to determine what is best for their children without infringement. We declare teachers shall be hired who set a good example and display integrity in their classroom. We decree teachers' unions shall maintain a righteous agenda. We prophesy that the Bible and prayer are welcome in the classroom and that the Pledge of Allegiance shall once again be taught and recited. We decree educational tax reforms and benefits are enacted for families who choose private education and homeschooling options. We declare a complete overhaul and reform of the educational systems of this nation in Jesus' Name!

SCRIPTURE

> *In everything set them an example by doing what is good. In your teaching show integrity, seriousness and soundness of speech that cannot be condemned, so that those who oppose you may be ashamed because they have nothing bad to say about us* (Titus 2:7-8 NIV).

WORD OF ENCOURAGEMENT

Not enough can be said about the damage that has been caused through the systems of education in this country.

The decline in morals is evident from school boards to teachers and just about every type of educator. The determined agenda by many schools around the country to indoctrinate our children with antibiblical, socialist, and immoral content is simply unacceptable. The devil knows to go after the young, and that is why the schools are one of his key targets. It's time for decent American citizens and Christians everywhere to stand up for our sons and daughters and not allow the secularized school systems to pervert the up-and-coming generations. Checks and balances need to be put in place so that teachers and the various boards of education do not have the unrestrained autonomy to teach certain subjects that have no business in the classroom.

As parents, grandparents, or simply as concerned citizens and believers, we can effect great change in education, not only by being involved but through targeted prayer! Let's decree a divine reform in education!

BIBLICAL MARRIAGE UPHELD

We decree that traditional and biblical marriage shall be upheld and defended in the United States of America. We emphasize God's definition of marriage as being a holy covenant between one man and one woman. We break the power of all manner of counterfeit unions and declare they cannot redefine or share in the definition of marriage as established by God. In Jesus' Name, we bind demons of lust, perversion, and immorality that seek to form homosexual and depraved unions that God has said are an abomination. We prophesy that all legislation promoting a falsified view or example of marriage shall not be upheld. We say that churches and pastors shall stand for the truth regarding biblical marriage and shall not fall into society's pressure to deviate from it. We say that no person, lawmaker, government official, or judge shall infringe upon the constitutional right of the Church to uphold and maintain the sanctity of marriage. We say that believers and Christian businesses shall be allowed to follow their own convictions regarding marriage and shall not be sued and persecuted for their beliefs. We declare an awakening comes upon our nation to stand for biblical marriage and that the covenant of marriage shall be upheld, in Jesus' Name!

SCRIPTURE

So God created man in his own image, in the image of God created he him; male and female created he them (Genesis 1:27 KJV).

Therefore shall a man leave his father and his mother, and shall cleave unto his wife: and they shall be one flesh (Genesis 2:24 KJV).

WORD OF ENCOURAGEMENT

God established marriage, and there is no other version of it beyond what He determined, which is that marriage is a holy covenant between one man and one woman. Yet some people, in the lust of their flesh, attempt to redefine God's definition of marriage demanding that it include any combination of individuals who decide to engage in a sensual relationship. This obviously has opened the door to a horrible "anything goes" ideology. However, since these other unions do not follow God's pattern for marriage, they are counterfeits. A great deal of effort has been made by progressives to not only try and hijack the sanctity of marriage according to the Bible, but to also persecute anyone who upholds God's standard of marriage. They are applying extreme measures that demand unquestioned compliance by everyone, not allowing anyone to maintain their own convictions or beliefs.

This growing trend is even being embraced in some churches and denominations nowadays and is an urgent matter of prayer! Only a few decades ago we would have never imagined the battle over the basic understanding of marriage would be so intensely challenged in our country. Prayer regarding this issue not only affects the spirit realm but reaffirms within us God's truth about biblical marriage in the face of opposition!

THE GREAT AWAKENING SHALL ARISE

DECLARATION

We decree that a divine awakening shall cover our nation. We prophesy that hearts and minds shall be awakened to God and receptive to salvation through Jesus Christ. We declare that people everywhere become open and desirous to hear the Word of God. We say that those who are resistant and committed to spreading evil ideologies, false religions, and sinful lifestyles shall be brought to the light and their wicked intentions shall be visible for all to see. We declare that every hardened heart begins to see the light and becomes open to God. We say that the light of the Lord shall shine upon cities, states, regions, and governments, and those who sit in darkness shall see the light. We speak a great awakening upon the backslidden church in America and we prophesy, "Awake, O sleeper!" We prophesy that the sleeping church arises and takes her rightful place. We command a new fervor, energy, and initiative to come upon every believer and church to fulfill their God-given purpose and heavenly assignment. We declare the greatest harvest of souls that our nation has ever witnessed shall manifest, and the Lord shall receive the precious fruit of the earth. We decree the season of heavenly awakening is upon us and that the time is now for the Great Awakening to arise!

SCRIPTURE

> *But their evil intentions will be exposed when the light shines on them, for the light makes every-thing visible. This is why it is said, "Awake, O sleeper, rise up from the dead, and Christ will give you light"* (Ephesians 5:13-14 NLT).

WORD OF ENCOURAGEMENT

In the church environment, we hear the term "awak-ening" used quite often to emphasize the dire need for hardened hearts to become open to the Lord and for backslidden believers to repent and return to God. We also use the term to emphasize the need for the believers in our country to willingly pay any price in order to stand for the Gospel and defend biblical truth.

What we must realize is that this type of great awakening must divinely come from God. We can't manufacture it. It happens in a way that no human can take the credit. When Jesus first began His earthly ministry, the region of Galilee, which was filled with darkness, became witness to the light (see Matt. 4:12-16). That region began to see and respond to the light and masses came to Jesus. This is the kind of awakening we must pray for in America! We can ask God to cause hearts and minds that were otherwise hardened to miraculously become receptive. We see countless examples of God doing this in the Bible, and we must pray that this same divine awakening will cover our land. Undoubtedly, the last days will be marked by a mass awakening, and we shall surely see that in the United States! Let's decree that the greatest awakening we have ever seen arises!

DECLARATION OVER LOCAL AND STATE GOVERNMENT

DECLARATION

We decree that local and state governments in this nation shall work for the prosperity and good welfare of their people. They shall enact bills and laws that are beneficial and that do not detract from the ability of people to build prosperous and godly lives. We say that local officials who are negligent and self-serving shall not be elected to or positioned in office. In the Name of Jesus, we bind demonic efforts to elect and position those who are determined to further leftist and socialist agendas in their cities, states, and townships. We decree a removal of governors and officials who are corrupt, dishonest, or involved in bribery for personal gain. We say that governors, mayors, city council members, and all other elected officials shall fulfill their oaths in integrity, with servitude and responsibility. We decree that they shall stand up in their rightful authority against all attempted overreaches by the federal government. We prophesy that citizens shall be committed to support and vote for honorable candidates in their local districts so their municipalities will be blessed. We declare governmental leaders of integrity shall have sufficient funding to keep their promises and further righteous causes. We say that God-fearing officials shall be positioned who shall boldly defend God's Word, pray during their meetings and public addresses, and unashamedly honor the Name of Jesus Christ. We decree that local and state governments of righteousness shall arise in the land!

SCRIPTURE

And work for the peace and prosperity of the city where I sent you into exile. Pray to the Lord for it, for its welfare will determine your welfare (Jeremiah 29:7 NLT).

WORD OF ENCOURAGEMENT

So often we get focused on national governmental officials and we overlook the importance of our local governments and how they impact our lives on a more direct level. Many people are unaware of what goes on in their state capital, city hall, or the agenda set forth during council meetings and so forth. And while we need to be involved on a civil level, we need to seriously pray for these localized branches.

The verse provides insights on what to pray regarding our cities and towns, directing us to specifically pray for peace and prosperity. Experiencing this in our local districts involves praying for the right governmental officials who are committed to furthering that type of environment. They need to be those who are not deceitful and self-serving, who are not going to let themselves be dragged into the common political cesspool of false narratives that often determines the priority focus of a large number of civic leaders. They feel the pressure to follow along with extreme special interests because they don't want to receive backlash for standing up for what's right. We need governors and leaders truly committed to their city's well-being, because when the city is well ordered the lives of the citizens who live there will prosper and live in peace!

PRAYER FOR LAW ENFORCEMENT

DECLARATION

We decree that the members of the law enforcement agencies and police departments in the United States of America are surrounded by the angels of the Lord. We prophesy that they will not be harmed while performing their duties in effort to keep our streets safe and neighborhoods secure. In Jesus' Name, we break the power of the violent that would attempt to assault and commit murder against our police officers. We say that every police officer shall be kept from evil, and their lives shall be protected. We bind the workers of lawlessness whose intent is to vandalize law enforcement facilities and discredit police officers. In Jesus' Name, we prophesy that federal and state governments shall not be able to weaponize law enforcement agents against civilians. We speak peace to the minds of every police officer and declare that they shall not suffer from emotional trauma and stress associated with their line of work. We declare God's peace and blessing over their families and say they shall not be fearful. We prophesy that the police of our nation shall receive increased funding to further excellence of training and professionalism. We declare they shall receive support from their cities and communities. We say that our men and women in law enforcement shall perform their duties professionally and shall be respected in return. We decree law enforcement across this nation shall be protected and kept safe in Jesus' Name!

SCRIPTURE

> *Deliver me, O Lord, from the evil man: preserve me from the violent man; which imagine mischiefs in their heart; continually are they gathered together for war* (Psalm 140:1-2 KJV).

WORD OF ENCOURAGEMENT

Police officers in this increasingly lawless culture often receive a considerable amount of backlash and criticism. Unfortunately, many people, particularly on the left, ignore the fact the police do a great deal more than just enforce the law. They also rescue lives from danger on countless levels, which always seems to be overlooked.

The media and special interest groups are always quick to jump in and misconstrue any perceived errors or mishandling on the part of law enforcement in an effort to stir public outcry. These segments of society tend to regularly defend the actions of criminals over their victims. They are eager to attack the brave men and women of law enforcement who work to save innocent lives from being harmed by these dangerous individuals.

As Christians we recognize the intense pressure our police officers are up against from public opinion, in addition to the dangers that they face every single day on the job. We realize the role law enforcement plays in keeping a well-structured society intact, something America has enjoyed more than many other countries. Praying God's blessing over law enforcement is so needed right now. We can include praying that outlandish claims by anti-police groups will be viewed factually and not gain traction. Nearly every police officer is pleased when someone lets them know they are appreciated and also being prayed for. Let's lift them up through prayer!

OVERTURNING OF EVIL LAWS AND LEGISLATION

DECLARATION

We decree that evil laws that have been enacted in this nation shall be overturned in Jesus' Name! We prophesy that statues and civic orders protecting immoral lifestyles and conduct will be replaced by that which is moral. We declare every law that restricts the liberty and involvement of the Lord's Church in society and government shall be eliminated in the Name of Jesus. We break the power of every mindset, by officials or the public, that is holding on to regulations, measures, and codes that are antibiblical and unconstitutional. We say the population opens it eyes to every law on the books that tramples the will of the people from pursuing a godly and decent way of life, and we declare that these laws shall be withdrawn. We say that every executive order or mandate that protects and advances an unreasonable few, while infringing upon and endangering others, will be immediately dismissed. We say that every unconstitutional law on record shall once again be reviewed and found objectionable by the courts and society. We prophesy a mass review and exposure on a state and federal level of hidden laws that are not beneficial or were devised with malicious intent. All laws and orders that are vile, wrong, or obscene will be rejected, not accepted. Laws that harm the children or manipulate the poor and needy will be removed immediately. Every such wicked law embedded in other laws on record shall be extracted and overturned. We decree an immediate and extensive overturning of evil laws and legislation across this land, in Jesus' Name!

SCRIPTURE

> *Woe to those who enact unjust statutes and to those who constantly record harmful decisions, so as to deprive the needy of justice and rob the poor among My people of their rights, so that widows may be their spoil and that they may plunder the orphans* (Isaiah 10:1-2 NASB).

> *To do justice and judgment is more acceptable to the Lord than sacrifice* (Proverbs 21:3 KJV).

WORD OF ENCOURAGEMENT

When Roe v. Wade was overruled by the Supreme Court as unconstitutional, demonstrating that it should have never passed on a federal level, it was a monumental moment. It reminded us as Christians that nothing, even that which has been around for decades, is set in stone. Anything can change in an instant, and it should serve as a strength to us that no wicked law is permanent and that it can be reviewed and further challenged.

The Scripture in Isaiah is a clear reminder that unjust statues are being upheld on shaky ground. It reveals that woe comes to those who enact unjust statutes and decide on laws that are harmful. God doesn't take it lightly when authorities put orders in place that abuse people. This is why the Scripture says it is woeful for them! It shows us that which they institute can and will change and be replaced by better. It's also important not to assume that because we are in the end times laws will only become more evil. Just like with Roe v. Wade, new moral and decent laws will continue to be passed while evil laws are overturned!

REVIVAL OF PRAYER!

We decree a revival of dedicated and celebrated prayer shall arise in the United States of America. We declare that the National Day of Prayer shall be honored by the president, Congress, and all governmental branches on a federal, state, and local level. We decree public prayer shall return to society in workplaces and schools. We say that churches shall begin to pray with fresh fervor. They will call out to God and prioritize prayer above all other programs and plans. We declare churches shall be known as houses of powerful prayer over being known as social gathering places. We break the power of all demonic resistance against genuine prayer. Rituals and counterfeit ceremonies conducted through false religion, satanic practices, or in the name of any entity other than the Name of Jesus Christ shall be rejected as an imitation and not be recognized as genuine prayer. We say that all atheistic roadblocks to biblical prayer in the public square shall be overcome and every hindrance destroyed. We call forth revivals that shall emphasize the importance and the power of prayer. We declare that a passionate prayer expression shall be birthed and restored in prayer groups, worship gatherings, and other events. We decree that this nation shall be known as a nation of prayer!

SCRIPTURE

And said unto them, It is written, My house shall be called the house of prayer; but ye have made it a den of thieves (Matthew 21:13 KJV).

WORD OF ENCOURAGEMENT

To the chagrin of some, America has a Christian heritage. It was founded on biblical principles with Jesus Christ as a central theme. Our nation by and large has had a strong church-attending population over the decades with many families at least owning or acknowledging the Bible. Our dollar bills still say, "In God We Trust." Scriptures and the Ten Commandments are displayed and inscribed upon the walls of many government buildings. Unless one is determined to do so, you can't ignore the foundation that helped form our great nation. The United States also honors its specific National Day of Prayer on the first Thursday of each May, with congressional law calling upon the president to issue a proclamation inviting people to pray. Prayer is part of our heritage, and we need prayer more than ever.

As Christians, we not only recognize the need for prayer, but we also know that the Church needs a revival of strong prayer and intercession. In accordance with Jesus' words, we need church houses to once again become houses of prayer rather than just places to gather for coffee and a short inspirational message. Our nation needs prayer by those who truly know how to pray and appeal to Heaven for our land. A prayer revival begins with us, the Church. Yes, many are praying, but let's believe that a fiery revival of prayer will be ignited across America!

Justice Served upon Workers of Evil

Declaration

We decree that those who are dedicated to work wicked acts upon and against this nation shall formally be brought to justice. In Jesus' Name, we decree they shall be cut off from their ability to concoct evil and criminal deeds under the table using bribery, deceit, forgery, false character defamations, violence, misconduct, and shady deals. We declare an exposure to all who craft such wickedness, and we say they shall be held liable under the full authority of the law. We pray for there to be those who shall repent of their evil acts and turn to the Lord Jesus Christ, but we say that the unrepentant shall be held accountable and removed from carrying out their plans to destroy this country. We prophesy that their descendants shall be unable to further their corruption to the next generation. We declare justice and recompense for the Lord's Church and the innocent who have suffered at the hands of the wicked and their treasonous acts. We speak preservation upon the saints in the United States, and we say that they shall be approved of the Lord and He shall keep them from evil. May due process be served upon workers of iniquity and may the righteous be upheld and exonerated in our land, in Jesus' Name!

SCRIPTURE

For the Lord loves justice; he will not forsake his saints. They are preserved forever, but the children of the wicked shall be cut off (Psalm 37:28 ESV).

I have seen a wicked, ruthless man, spreading himself like a green laurel tree. But he passed away, and behold, he was no more; though I sought him, he could not be found (Psalm 37:35-36 ESV).

WORD OF ENCOURAGEMENT

Nothing can be more infuriating than seeing someone get away with evil. We have a justice system in our country for a reason, and when used properly it's a system of checks and balances designed to prevent abuses. Nevertheless, we have seen the evildoer's actions being helped and covered up by other evildoers time and time again. We've seen judges who use the law to sentence those whom they deem a political enemy. We've seen the reports of governors, leaders, or members of Congress who have used the system to their advantage or financial gain while unleashing all-out attacks on any of their opponents whom they deem to have done the same.

It's difficult to sort out, but one thing is clear—God loves justice! At some point, things will shake out and the wicked will be cut off, and that doesn't just apply to the end of the age. We have to remember throughout Scripture there were many situations when it seemed that the evildoers had the upper hand and were not being held accountable for their actions. However, their day of justice came eventually. As we pray, let's stand strong in the fact that God will ensure that justice is delivered upon the evil we are seeing. In the Scripture passage it says that one can actually wake up one day, look around, and not be able to locate the evildoers of yesterday. Our prayers can bring a stop to the unrestrained advancement of those who work wicked deeds, and we can see justice served.

Ungodly Agendas and Ideologies Shall Fail!

We decree that man-made agendas and ideologies shall fail. We prophesy that plans and beliefs built upon humanism, atheism, selfism, and pride shall be destroyed by the power of God. Every philosophy, idea, and agenda erected through demonic influence is broken in the Name of Jesus! We bind socialism, totalitarianism, communism, and false religion. We take authority over every mind-binding demon that would confuse people's minds causing them to misinterpret and twist the truth or the facts. We bind the forked tongue of the corrupt and say they cannot lure people into erroneous political doctrines and tenets. We say that woke agendas and ungodly programs shall be halted and unable to move forward. We release that which is good upon this nation! In the Name of Jesus, we loose a spirit of blessing, goodness, kindness, and agendas that are for the well-being and godly justice of the people. We prophesy that ideas and principles shall be developed which shall supply helpful solutions. Those solutions will be passed through Congress and the Oval Office without being stonewalled and vetoed. We declare a divine outpouring of humility and a turning to God for answers, and we call for a mass shift toward righteousness in people's beliefs. We decree every ungodly belief system shall utterly fail in Jesus' Name!

SCRIPTURE

He has told you, O man, what is good; and what does the Lord require of you but to do justice, and to love kindness, and to walk humbly with your God? (Micah 6:8 ESV)

WORD OF ENCOURAGEMENT

The verse above is a short summary of the character God expects to reside inside every human being. Obviously it doesn't, but this verse is a clear address from God to humanity. Yet rather than good we are often seeing people turn toward hatred and mean-spirited ways. Many who scream for justice are the most egregious instigators of injustice. They demand from others what they refuse to give in return. They are devoid of the most basic forms of human kindness but rather marked by pride and self-ism. Using threats, they work to impose their extreme and false beliefs upon others. They shake their fist at God in defiance to retain the evil things they want to abide by.

Undoubtedly these examples are all too familiar in our society, but what can be done? It begins with a divine out-pouring across the nation that causes people to turn from such behaviors. It also begins with those who are already willing to follow the principles found in Micah 6:8. If we would walk humbly with our God, our beliefs would be rightly aligned. Loving justice according to God's stan-dard would change what people do and the ideologies they embrace. It would shift how we treat our fellow man. It would change the actions of leadership in government. Causing this to happen requires supernatural intervention, but we can definitely pray for a failure of man-made ide-ologies, agendas, and attitudes so that we can see the good arise. We can declare the godly things replace the ungodly, and people everywhere will believe differently and follow what God requires.

PRAYER FOR THE CONGRESS

DECLARATION

We decree that the rule of God rests over the Congress of the United States of America. We prophesy that God's throne directs its paths and agenda. As the members of Congress convene, we decree they shall discuss, collaborate, and plan according to righteousness. In the Name of Jesus, we break the power of every evil spirit that would attempt to dictate the House of Representatives and the Senate. We prophesy that every legislative bill that furthers wickedness shall be voted down. We say that our elected officials shall represent the will of the people consistent with honor and integrity. They shall not be swayed toward special interests characterized by an antichrist spirit. We declare that congressional members and senators shall be elected and placed in office who are law-abiding, honorable, and committed to our nation's sovereignty. We prophesy unity over our Congress and declare it will uphold and defend the decency of the law and the Constitution. We declare peace and order in the house and senate chambers, and we say that each member shall exhibit manners and professionalism consistent with orderly conduct. We prophesy that prayer shall be prioritized in both the house and senate chambers. We pray protection and peace over the Capitol building, and we command evil spirits to depart the premises in the Name of Jesus! We say that the Congress of this nation shall be operated as intended by its founding members and nothing shall interfere with its purpose, in Jesus' Name!

SCRIPTURE

God reigns over the nations; God sits on his holy throne. The princes of the peoples gather as the people of the God of Abraham. For the shields of the earth belong to God; he is highly exalted! (Psalm 47:8-9 ESV)

WORD OF ENCOURAGEMENT

There is no doubt that the United States Congress is among the most important elements of our government and serves as the legislative body for this nation. It was strategically designed to be a safeguard against tyranny with its 535 total voting members (435 in the house and 100 in the senate) representing the people from all 50 states. Our founding fathers intended the elected members of both chambers to be a voice for their constituents regarding what is voted into law. We should be thankful for this body of our government that provides checks and balances regarding what happens in our nation. Sadly, we have too often seen house and senate members emphasize their personal agenda rather than that of the people, and too often their efforts have been directed toward evil. We have seen the scales tipping in the direction of those who want to bring harm to our country.

Yet the Bible reminds us that it's God who reigns over the nations. National leaders may gather with evil intentions, but we can gather and intercept their plans through the power of prayer and prophetic decree. Praying and declaring over the Congress of this nation should be a dedicated and ongoing assignment for every Christian. We can shift this nation for the better through undergirding the United States Congress in prayer!

INFLUENTIAL PASTORS AND CHURCHES

DECLARATION

We decree that bold, powerful, and anointed churches shall rise into a place of influence across this land. We prophesy that pastors shall arise with God's heart, agenda, and anointing. We declare pastors will emerge who are not afraid to address important issues in the culture and who will not bend toward the worldly trends in society. We say that these churches shall prosper financially, succeed, build buildings, expand territory, and grow in attendance. May they carry influence on the airways and may their online viewership explode in growth. We declare pastors and churches shall begin to take their rightful place in government, schools, homes, entertainment, and media. We prophesy they will be well received and invited to have a role in all sectors of society in the United States of America. They shall have a voice into our nation's political leaders and be able to encourage a restoration of prayer and biblical values. We declare a boldness arises among pastors and church leaders to stand up for truth. We decree they shall preach the full counsel of God's Word and not avoid a command for righteousness. We say that churches who have deviated from biblical truth shall lose their influence in this nation. May healthy churches be established, which shall govern the flock of God with love, purity, and order. We say this nation shall see powerful churches arise and people everywhere will return to the house of God in Jesus' Name!

SCRIPTURE

> *Turn, O backsliding children, saith the Lord; for I am married unto you: and I will take you one of a city, and two of a family, and I will bring you to Zion: and I will give you pastors according to mine heart, which shall feed you with knowledge and understanding* (Jeremiah 3:14-15 KJV).

WORD OF ENCOURAGEMENT

Most older adults can recall a time in our nation's history when the majority of families attended church. It was a priority on Sunday morning, and very few things interfered with this important commitment. Slowly we have seen Sunday morning replaced by recreation, sports, and other activities and the church's influence in society began to wane. To try and keep interest alive, many pastors turned to creating relevant activities and belief systems that are more in line with the direction of society than the Bible. Many pastors and church leaders also spent less time ensuring their voice was inserted in the political places of influence; thus, today's church is largely absent from it.

What is important to understand is that many of our nation's founders were born-again believers and some were also ministers. In their day, pastors were deeply immersed in what took place in government. It was considered important to have a biblical worldview regarding political matters. Obviously, so much has changed in this regard, and we need to pray that God will once again raise up churches and leaders who have influence in this way. We need pastors and church leaders who will not avoid being involved or speaking up in the culture. It's time for the church's role to be brought back to its rightful place in our nation! Let's declare it in Jesus' Name!

PEACE UPON THE STREETS!

DECLARATION

We decree peace to the streets of this nation! We break the power of violence, riots, restlessness, partying, carousing, and all criminal activity, in Jesus' Name. We declare our neighborhoods are free from drug abuse, intoxication, homelessness, kidnapping, rape, murder, human trafficking, and prostitution. We say our communities are free from accidents, emergencies, tragedies, and suicides. We prophesy that the night hours shall be marked by quietness and tranquility. Our daytime hours shall be calm, productive, and harmonious. We prophesy that our streets are free from danger and our children grow up and play in a safe environment. We decree that the businesses in our streets and neighborhoods can operate securely and without the threat of robbery, looting, or vandalism. We say our homes and property are free from thieves, vandals, and home invaders in the Name of Jesus! We speak peace over the weather, the land, wildlife, waterways, city utilities, and all buildings and structures, and we declare no occurrences of tragedy or calamity. We decree the streets of our cities, towns, and neighborhoods are granted the Lord's divine peace, and we shall live without fear in this nation. We speak peace upon our streets in America in Jesus' Name!

SCRIPTURE

> *I will grant peace in the land, and you will lie down and no one will make you afraid. I will remove wild beasts from the land, and the sword will not pass through your country* (Leviticus 26:6 NIV).

WORD OF ENCOURAGEMENT

One of the reasons we often don't see a change in how things are is because we become comfortable with status quo. We don't always perceive that just because something has been a certain way for a long time doesn't mean there shouldn't be change or there can't be change. When we look at our communities, regardless of what kind of neighborhood we live in, whether urban, suburban, or rural, we can't just remain tolerant of the wrong. We need to recognize that evil, whether it be directly from human behaviors or natural disaster, is spurred on by demon spirits. And while we need to be actively involved in changing what we can in our communities, we also have the power to bind up these evil forces and make a declaration of peace to the area where we live. We want our children to grow up in a safe environment that isn't marked by tragedy and danger.

Look at the community you live in and determine the areas where God's peace needs to be injected. Perhaps you live in a rural area marked by tornadoes. Speak that no tornado will be able to destroy your community in Jesus' Name! If you live in an urban area, declare that your neighborhood will not be marked by crime and violence. Let's not just accept whatever is expected in our particular locale or what might already be happening there. Let's decree the Lord's peace upon our streets and that we shall live safely without fear!

PROTECTION OF THE UNITED STATES CONSTITUTION

DECLARATION

We decree that the guiding principles of the Constitution of the United States of America and every amendment in the Bill of Rights shall be revered, valued, and upheld. We bind every attempt to remove and ignore the Bill of Rights and its solemn protections offered to every citizen. In Jesus' Name, we break the power of every demonic force that would censor our right to free speech, our liberty to assemble and worship God, or that would attempt to rescind our right to bear arms. We decree the amendments are upheld, affording people the right to live free from invasion, seizure, and tyrannical punishment by the government. We decree our right to have due process and effective legal representation of the law shall be honorably upheld. We decree the rights of individual citizens and states under the Constitution shall not be illegally usurped by the federal government. We prophesy that the preamble to the Declaration of Independence shall be honored, declaring that all men are created equal and have the right to life, liberty, and the pursuit of happiness, and that the government's responsibility is to protect these rights. We declare that the Constitution of the United States shall remain our counsel for the good of every citizen and shall be properly interpreted and acted upon. We declare those who would abuse, misinterpret, distort, or falsify our Constitution for wicked intentions shall be exposed and brought to justice. We decree the entirety of the Constitution shall remain intact and will not be overlooked or deliberately ignored. We call upon God's hand of protection over the United States Constitution, in Jesus' Name!

SCRIPTURE

Where no counsel is, the people fall: but in the multitude of counsellors there is safety (Proverbs 11:14 KJV).

WORD OF ENCOURAGEMENT

Anyone who truly loves our country knows the value of the United States Constitution and just how much protection it offers every person to live in peace and in safety from government control. The spirit behind it was to prevent government from abuse and inflicting excess control and restrictions upon the people. It's not meant to offer one the right to be lawless but rather the liberty to pursue an orderly and successful life as they understand it. It was designed to keep the government from restricting our right to honor the Lord. It is not a document that prevents us as Christians from speaking into the government. However, we are seeing an increasing populace of people and political figures who want to undermine our Constitution so they can further an evil agenda. If there was ever an important time in history to be educated on what is written in the Bill of Rights and the remaining amendments of the Constitution as a whole, it's now! We must also pray against those who want to ignore these guiding documents or misinterpret their intent. These founding documents have been the counsel that has made this nation successful, and we must pray over them, protect their integrity, and stand up for them in truth. Let's decree and pray for God's divine protection to rest over the United States Constitution!

HONOR OF THE MILITARY AND VETERANS

We decree our military personnel and veterans receive the appropriate honor and benefits for their service. We prophesy that they are respected in society and their well-being is defended by our government officials. We declare safety over our military personnel and families abroad, and we declare they are protected during all practices, drills, and operations, in the Name of Jesus. We say they shall be fearless against their enemies and shall perform their duties with confidence and assurance. We bind all frivolous and senseless uses of our troops overseas to deploy them in wars and conflicts that have no purpose or value. We speak over our veterans, and we say they shall receive the care they deserve, and their needs shall be met and prioritized. We decree that veteran care centers, hospitals, and facilities shall be managed with the utmost excellence and all such places that do not meet quality standards shall be investigated and overhauled. We prophesy that all branches of the

United States military shall uphold their honor for this nation and will maintain a moral code of decency. We declare our military will not incorporate absurd ideologies that detract from its primary purpose to defend the national security of this country. We speak strength over our military, and we declare elected officials shall invest in our military to make it strong, stable, and the greatest fighting force in the world. We pray for God's blessing and mighty hand of power to rest upon the military of the United States of America, in Jesus' Name!

SCRIPTURE

> *He will say to them, "Listen to me, all you men of Israel! Do not be afraid as you go out to fight your enemies today! Do not lose heart or panic or tremble before them. For the Lord your God is going with you! He will fight for you against your enemies, and he will give you victory!"* (Deuteronomy 20:3-4 NLT).

WORD OF ENCOURAGEMENT

It's clear that one of the key elements that has made this nation stand out is our military. It remains the top military in the world and there is no doubt it's because God's hand has been upon it. One of the elements that makes the United States military special is it's a volunteer force allowing members to choose to join and to fight for the freedoms that this country has heralded worldwide. Our military personnel have, for the most part, been offered benefits that many armies around the globe simply do not have.

Unfortunately, there are always those, whether in government or part of society, who don't value our members in uniform and the price they have paid for our freedom. They devalue and degrade our service personnel. We see politicians cut military spending while handing arms to our enemies. We have also seen branches of the military bow to the pressure to embrace woke ideologies. This has been a tremendous distraction from their primary mission. We need to pray for our military that it will continue to stand for God and country, but also that God's hand will be upon our service men and women who are committed to the good of this nation!

MORAL DECENCY
ESTABLISHED AND RESTORED

DECLARATION

We decree a moral righteousness and decency is established in the United States of America. We prophesy that men and women across this land shall stand for what is morally honorable and right. We declare a movement toward modesty, purity, and virtue shall arise and shift the culture toward good. In Jesus' Name, we break the demonic powers of sexual perversion, lust, adultery, gender dysphoria, fornication, incest, and homosexuality. We say that styles, entertainment, businesses, and education shall begin to move toward an expression of decency and prudence. We command a removal of immoral print material, programming, websites, advertisements, and signs, in Jesus' Name. We say there shall be a removal of pornographic content online. Internet predators shall be caught and brought to justice. We decree that towns, communities, and cities shall legislate toward a righteous moral standard and shall reject that which opens the door for evil to prey upon the innocent. We say there shall be a movement to herald righteous principles among young people who will not bow to peer pressure. We say there shall arise a new sexual revolution that shall return the culture to biblical morals and that will reject looseness and lewdness. We decree a moral decency shall be established and restored in this nation!

SCRIPTURE

> *Righteousness exalteth a nation: but sin is a reproach to any people* (Proverbs 14:34 KJV).

WORD OF ENCOURAGEMENT

It's sad to see how much society has regressed regarding sexual morals. The sexual revolution of the 1960s opened the way for a lot of evil. Before it, we once grieved over the growing stats on teen pregnancy, which eventually escalated into millions of abortions. The way was opened for fornication and even adultery to become accepted and normal. From there we saw society embrace new forms of sexual lewdness through bisexual and homosexual agendas. The trend even affected churches as pastors sold out to the pressure and decided to perform homosexual unions. The world worsened with the introduction of the Internet as pornographic images invaded computers everywhere. Now it's hit a new pinnacle of evil with transgenderism and drag shows preying upon innocent children. We could not have imagined a handful of years ago school children being coaxed with "gender affirmation" by schoolteachers or doctors mutilating the bodies of children with puberty blockers and gender related surgeries. In some states, parents are threatened with losing their children if they interfere.

We must intercede and pray for a revival of moral decency to return to this nation! The Bible says sin is a reproach in any nation and the payment of sin is death (see Rom. 6:23). People want to think that this type of unrestrained immoral behavior can continue without consequence, but we are already seeing the consequences as lives are being ruined because of sexual sin. Let's pray and believe for a sexual revolution in reverse, one that reverses the damage done but that also commands a moral standard of righteousness to return to our nation!

HONOR FOR OUR FLAG

DECLARATION

We decree that the flag of the United States shall be honored and respected. We say that it shall be revered as the symbol that unites us as a nation and as a people. We prophesy that people everywhere will display and fly it proudly. May there be a renewed understanding of its meaning and how it represents that we are one nation under God, a nation of liberty and justice for all. We say that the flag shall not be used as a symbol of protest. We declare that those who would take actions against our flag to misrepresent its purpose, disgrace, trample, or burn it shall be rebuked for their disrespectful actions. In Jesus' Name, we decree there shall be no counterfeit or substitute flags created, displayed, or accepted. May every citizen see the flag as a symbol of freedom and a banner for those who have fought and died to preserve it. May it be flown in the face of our enemies and as a rallying call to every American to defend our interests at home and abroad. We prophesy that schools shall once again recite and print the Pledge of Allegiance. We say the National Anthem shall be sung and played aloud at gatherings, sporting, and political events nationwide. We declare that businesses shall honor our flag and display it on their properties, print material, and web pages. May the flag be displayed in homes and churches. We call for our flag to be honored by every citizen who values what it stands for in our great nation, in Jesus' Name!

SCRIPTURE

> *But you have raised a banner for those who fear you—a rallying point in the face of attack* (Psalm 60:4 NLT).

WORD OF ENCOURAGEMENT

Every country has a flag. Its purpose is to act as a symbol of unity and to show that one treasures the nation where they live. Our flag here in the United States is to represent that we are a free republic and that men and women gave their lives to defend what we enjoy every day. This is why we honor it, defend it, and respect our flag. We remember the moments when this beautiful symbol was laid upon the coffins of our service members, and it reminded us to give thanks for their sacrifice. This is why using the flag for protest or in any other disrespectful manner is so egregiously offensive. The flag is the one symbol that reminds us to rise above our many differences and remember, at the end of the day, we are all Americans. We live here, we do business here, and we interact here as people. Our flag serves to remind us that we are blessed as a country in ways many others are not.

Undoubtedly, a new respect for the flag needs to return to our culture. Many have used it for the wrong means, and many leftists are removing it from all mention or expression. There needs to be a pushback by patriotic Americans who understand what our flag stands for and who are thankful for what it represents. We need to display our flags and national colors proudly. We need to remember the Pledge of Allegiance and our National Anthem. As Christians, we can pray that these national symbols will be preserved because we know God loves this nation and He raised it up as a beacon of light around the world. Let's declare a new honor for our flag!

UNITY OF THE SAINTS

DECLARATION

We decree that the Body of Christ across this nation shall be unified. We say that they shall be of one heart, one mind, and one purpose. We declare that the people of God shall choose to emphasize the important elements upon which they agree and not capitalize on where they don't agree. We declare believers shall walk in love with one another and not be drawn into arguments, debates, and criticisms. We place a restraint upon online bickering and disagreements that serve to destroy rather than edify. We prophesy that God's people shall stand as one and we break the power of division, betrayal, gossip, and disunity, in Jesus' Name. We break the power of church splits and divisive lawsuits among brethren, in Jesus' Name. We loose a spirit of forgiveness, mercy, and meekness in the Body of Christ, and we decree that offenses shall be extinguished by the power of the Holy Spirit. We say that believers in America shall remain unified regarding the authority of the Bible as the inspired Word of God. In Jesus' Name, we break the influence of those who would act as counterfeit Christians or pastors who deny and distort the truth of Scripture. May the saints of God stand unified upon the truth of the cross, resurrection, and the only way to salvation through Christ, and may they not be drawn into false ideologies and doctrines. We decree that the company of believers in this nation stands unified in Jesus' Name!

SCRIPTURE

Behold, how good and how pleasant it is for brethren to dwell together in unity! (Psalm 133:1 KJV)

By this shall all men know that ye are my disciples, if ye have love one to another (John 13:35 KJV).

WORD OF ENCOURAGEMENT

It has been reported that Adolf Hitler once said that Christians and churches interfering with his agenda was not a concern and his reasoning was because Christians are divided. It's sad that the wicked can see this while many believers cannot and thus continue in their strife and division. We have seen many instances even today in which secular media has capitalized upon the division in the church to make Christians a laughingstock. They have joyfully reported on the horrendous church splits, lawsuits among brethren, and now on the online bickering that has enflamed Christendom. In many ways, online comments have allowed church strife and poor behavior among believers to be displayed on a whole new level. None of this represents the Body of Christ properly.

Jesus made it clear that the world will know we are His by how we love each other. When the Bible says it is pleasant when brethren live in unity, that's because unity is peaceful. Strife is stressful; it hurts good people and is a terrible testimony to a world already filled with strife and brokenness. If we're going to be the answer to a hurting nation, we must become unified. We won't always agree, but can we not focus on where we do? The Bible gives more directives about covering each other's shortcomings than it does about calling out each other's wrongs. It's an urgent time to pray for the unity of the saints in America. Our nation truly needs us to be one!

MIRACLES, SIGNS, AND WONDERS MANIFESTING!

We decree that signs, wonders, and miracles shall begin to manifest across this nation. We declare that the Church and the prophets shall arise and prophesy. Their words shall be filled with authoritative power and their prophetic words shall undeniably manifest before all the world. We call for supernatural signs in the heavens and wonders in the earth that shall garner the attention of the secular media. We prophesy that they shall have to report about the signs that have come from God because they won't be able to deny them. We say there shall be the manifestation of angels that shall be witnessed in every region and state. We decree there shall be divine healings that shall shock the medical community causing them to turn to the Lord, and we declare a revival of documented creative miracles shall sweep across the United States. Like it was in the days of the Bible, we say the unjustly imprisoned, wrongfully indicted, and persecuted shall be divinely exonerated and released for all to see. We say there shall be heavenly visions and dreams among secular leaders, political figures, and influencers that shall be used to shift the direction of this country toward God. We say divine God encounters shall infiltrate homes, families, businesses, and schools, which shall spark great revival. We prophesy a miraculous shift of finances to be taken from the wicked and transferred into the hands of the righteous. We declare the supernatural power of the Holy Spirit shall saturate churches, prayer gatherings, and worship services in the Name of Jesus. We prophesy that a great move of signs, wonders, and miracles shall blanket the United States of America!

SCRIPTURE

And it shall come to pass in the last days, saith God, I will pour out of my Spirit upon all flesh: and your sons and your daughters shall prophesy, and your young men shall see visions, and your old men shall dream dreams: and on my servants and on my handmaidens I will pour out in those days of my Spirit; and they shall prophesy: and I will shew wonders in Heaven above, and signs in

*the earth beneath; blood, and fire, and vapour of
smoke* (Acts 2:17-19 KJV).

WORD OF ENCOURAGEMENT

If anything stands out in Scripture, it's the supernatural side of Almighty God! Page after page of the Bible describes His powerful intervention in the direst of circumstances. To ignore the miraculous attributes of God's character is to truly ignore God Himself. He wants to intervene with signs, wonders, and miracles for us!

One of the issues we have in our nation right now is many of God's people have forgotten that we serve a supernatural, miraculous God whose power is limitless. Many are looking at America as if it's irreparable and doomed. They can't believe that God can shift an entire nation in a short period of time or even in a day, yet we see this happen throughout the Bible! As we pray for this nation, let's call for God's divine intervention and believe there will be displays of miracles the world cannot ignore. It's time for signs and wonders to manifest!

OUR CHRISTIAN
HERITAGE PRESERVED

DECLARATION

We decree that the Christian and biblical heritage that
this nation was founded upon shall be preserved. We
say that the prayers and Scriptures displayed and inscribed upon our government buildings, courthouses,
monuments, and memorials shall be maintained, protected, and celebrated. This nation shall welcome signs,
images, and mottos that honor Jesus Christ as Lord. We
prophesy that the preeminence of Christian worship
and churches shall continue to be the way of life in the
United States. We say that prayer shall be welcomed
and allowed in public places. We decree our Christian
holidays shall be celebrated with their original titles
and meanings. We declare the inscription, "In God We
Trust" shall be preserved on our money. We prophesy
that the clauses and amendments of our Constitution
that were founded upon the Bible shall never be deleted,
in the Name of Jesus! We declare Christian education
shall ascend to a place of prominence and that biblical

principles shall be taught once again in our schools and universities. In Jesus' Name, we break the power of every atheistic and antichrist spirit that would attempt to destroy our Christian heritage as a country or delete the expression of Christianity from the culture. We bind all false religions and satanic worship from gaining interest or traction in Jesus Name! We decree that Christianity and the Bible shall be heralded as truth in America, and it shall never be removed!

SCRIPTURE

Blessed is the nation whose God is the Lord; and the people whom he hath chosen for his own inheritance (Psalm 33:12 KJV).

WORD OF ENCOURAGEMENT

The world loves to try and hide the fact that our nation's founders were students of the Bible and were intentional about weaving the Bible into the original fabric of this country. Their determination to ensure that God was honored and biblical principles were included in our creeds and documents is evident. Our most iconic buildings are inscribed with Bible verses and Christian images. The Ten Commandments have been displayed in countless courthouses, and most houses of worship are also Christian. You cannot ignore that our national heritage is in fact Christian at the core, and this is something we must wholeheartedly defend and assert!

It's no secret that wicked people are trying to destroy the godly legacy that founded this nation. Yet they can't see that our Christian heritage is the reason why America has been greatly blessed by God. They are doing all they can to strike down every Christian expression. Despite their efforts, Americans are pushing back and deciding they will pray in public and they will stand for biblical values. However, to keep our heritage secure we can't draw back and ignore the enemy's tactics in this regard. If every believer would arise as a defender of these truths about our country, it will be difficult for those with an atheistic or antichrist spirit to succeed. Let's decree that our nation's Christian heritage shall be honored and preserved in Jesus' Name!

POVERTY AND FAMINE DEFEATED

DECLARATION

We decree that the demonic spirits of poverty, lack, and famine in this nation shall be defeated in the Name of Jesus! We speak over the poor and destitute communities across this land, and we declare they begin to flourish and revitalize. We break the spirit of decay, decrease, and depreciation, and we say they are replaced with increase and growth. We declare that the homeless, the destitute, and the vagabond find stability and refuge. We say that the lazy, sluggard, wasteful, and idle person shall rise from their ways and seek new, responsible opportunities, purpose, and discipline. We prophesy that the working poor shall find gainful employment and the financial undergirding that they need. We decree that the sick, wounded, disabled, helpless, and weakened person shall receive resources and help from the Lord. We declare there shall be supply for the widow, widower, the single parent, the children, and for the abused. We prophesy that Christian-based help centers, food, and clothing pantries and shelters shall arise and succeed in meeting the needs of the poor across this land. We declare that politicians who manipulate the poor, ignore the impoverished, and abuse their power over them shall be removed. May reasonable programs be established that shall bring true help and ongoing resources to the needy. We prophesy that all intent by the government to further a spirit of poverty in this nation is bound in Jesus' Name! We decree lack and poverty are defeated in the United States of America!

SCRIPTURE

> *For thou hast been a strength to the poor, a strength to the needy in his distress, a refuge from the storm, a shadow from the heat, when the blast of the terrible ones is as a storm against the wall* (Isaiah 25:4 KJV).

WORD OF ENCOURAGEMENT

Jesus said the poor you will always have with you (see Matt. 26:11). People in need have always been part of every country and society, and America is no exception.

Fortunately, God has blessed this nation to be able to offer help to the poor in ways many other nations simply don't have. We have programs, shelters, and resources, both private and government-based, that help undergird people in destitute circumstances. Nevertheless, a spirit of poverty and lack is always seeking to devour and do all it can to increase the population of poor people in every country. We must remember that poverty is entirely demonic and nothing good comes from it. There are demons at work behind it, and we need to command their destroying power to be broken, in Jesus' Name!

We also need to pray for more Christian-based resources and programs to arise that can not only help the needy, but also show the way of salvation. We also need politicians and government-based programs that hurt the situation rather than help it to be replaced by something better. There is nothing wrong with government programs, but many political leaders don't manage these programs properly and thus aren't helping people or their communities at all. Let's believe for poverty, however it manifests, to be defeated in Jesus' Name!

THE SPIRIT OF FEAR AND TERROR IS BOUND!

DECLARATION

We decree that the spirit of fear and terror that would desire to invade America is bound, in Jesus' Name! We take authority over the demons that would cause all manner of alarm, pandemonium, and panic. We declare the people of this nation will not be drawn into scare tactics, uneasiness, or any type of public frenzy. We prophesy that the media, government, and foreign nations shall not be able to invade the United States with strategies, pandemics, and exercises that strike fear in the hearts of the public. We break the controlling power of international and domestic terrorism. We declare that Americans shall feel confident to go to and from their homes without dread. We break the power of paranoia from the hearts and minds of the people. We bind the fear of sicknesses, poisoning, hunger, financial loss, disaster, catastrophe, and violence against humanity. We declare people will not fear for their lives, for their families, or for their children. We say this nation is infused with a sense of peace and security from Heaven. We call for the Lord's supernatural covering of peace to envelop our cities, regions, and states. We speak assurance upon the people of God, and we say they shall be anointed to give hope in troubling times. We decree the spirit of terror cannot enact its evil agenda in this land, in Jesus' Name!

SCRIPTURE

Men's hearts failing them for fear, and for looking after those things which are coming on the earth: for the powers of Heaven shall be shaken (Luke 21:26 KJV).

For God hath not given us the spirit of fear; but of power, and of love, and of a sound mind (2 Timothy 1:7 KJV).

WORD OF ENCOURAGEMENT

The pandemic of 2020 revealed how easily the public can be drawn into a panic. We saw some of the most ridiculous efforts enacted in hopes of preventing the spread of disease. Even though many of these efforts made no logical sense, they were pushed and pressed regardless all because of utter fear. People incorporated rituals and practices they never would do otherwise simply because they were terrified. Even the Church was drawn in by it all. Fear among a populace can cause people to react in alarming ways and do things that make no sense and even sicken them. In fact, our verse says that in the last days, people's hearts will fail them because of fear. Their eyes will be so fixated on all that is happening, it seems they will literally die of heart failure! Being glued to the reports of terror is even easier nowadays with the availability of real-time information.

While we can't eliminate all disastrous circumstances in the world, we can by faith come against the spirit of terror trying to rob people of reason and an overall sense of peace. We can pray that the citizens of this nation will not be overwhelmed by anxiety that comes from the work of evil spirits. Because we are truly in the last days, it's important that we pray and decree against these spirits of fear and terror in America and declare that we will never be drawn in by them on such a mass level ever again, in Jesus' Name!

PROTECTION FOR THE CHILDREN

DECLARATION

We decree that the children and minors of the United States of America shall be protected by the hand of the Lord. We declare all abusers, predators, kidnappers, traffickers, murderers, and gangsters shall be stopped in advance, arrested, and imprisoned. We say never again will they be able to lay their wicked hands upon our children, in Jesus' Name. We declare all those who would lie, indoctrinate, and pressure our young people with evil shall be exposed and brought to justice. We decree that every program, facility, and ideology that targets minors and children with wrong shall be immediately eliminated. We bind the work of every charmer, seducer, and tempter that would lure children away from safety and righteousness. We declare online predators seeking minors shall be caught and sentenced, in Jesus' Name. We call for angelic reinforcements to cover our children! We declare that God's hand overshadows them and keeps them safe. We decree parents shall protect their sons and daughters and not leave them as prey to the culture of wickedness and worldliness. We declare the entertainment industry will be held accountable for the evils they present to the young generations. We say the children of this nation shall be esteemed as precious, and these who cannot defend themselves shall be fervently defended by parents, pastors, church leaders, teachers, government and public safety officials, medical professionals, and good citizens everywhere. May justice fall upon anyone who would cause one of our little ones to stumble, and we declare divine protection for our children, in Jesus' Name!

SCRIPTURE

And all thy children shall be taught of the Lord; and great shall be the peace of thy children (Isaiah 54:13 KJV).

Then said he unto the disciples, It is impossible but that offences will come: but woe unto him, through whom they come! It were better for him that a millstone were hanged about his neck, and he cast into the sea, than that he should offend one of these little ones (Luke 17:1-2 KJV).

WORD OF ENCOURAGEMENT

Seeing children and young people being mistreated is not only extremely heartbreaking, but cause for righteous anger. Nothing should cause more indignation than seeing innocent children deliberately harmed and abused. Jesus said those who abuse children would be better off being thrown into the ocean to their death (see Luke 17:2). His point was they have reached a point of such reprobate sin that they can't be rehabilitated.

What has been revealed recently about abuses of children is beyond alarming. While child abuse isn't new, what is newer is certain abuses are gaining ground as acceptable. Once trusted figures such as schoolteachers, doctors, and government agencies are promoting creative ways to prey upon children. Human trafficking is at an all-time high and seems to be largely dismissed. We as God's people, and all citizens, need to sound the alarm for justice, but we also need to truly intercede for God's protection upon our children!

We the People of the United States, in order to form a more perfect Union, establish Justice, insure domestic Tranquility, provide for the common defence, promote the general Welfare, and secure the Blessings of Liberty to ourselves and our Posterity, do ordain and establish this Constitution for the United States of America.

Article I.

Article II.

INTERNATIONAL SAFETY AND PEACE

DECLARATION

We decree that the citizens of the United States of America shall experience safety and peace when they travel abroad. We say that those who would harm Americans and the interests of its citizens around the world shall be interrupted from carrying out their intentions. We break the spirit of international terror, and we command its agenda to fail, in Jesus' Name. We speak safety over the transportation, housing, hotels, resorts, churches, towns, villages, and cities, and wherever United States citizens are present. We prophesy that innocent Americans shall not be kidnapped, imprisoned, or executed, in Jesus' Name! We prophesy safety over our military installations around the world, and we say that our service men and women and their families shall remain secure. We declare protection over every American missionary, and we say that no worker of violence can harm them. We decree prosperity, grace, and angelic covering over their work for the Kingdom of God overseas. We say no evil shall befall them and no plague shall come near their dwelling. We declare safety for every healthcare worker, contractor, teacher, disaster relief worker, rescuer, compassion giver, and ambassador working in other nations. We say no evil can touch them, and we bind the spirit of death and disaster from coming upon them, in Jesus' Name! We decree the State Department of this nation shall work effectively to ensure the safety of all Americans living and working abroad and shall not ignore the welfare of its citizens. We decree international safety and peace!

SCRIPTURE

> *Then shalt thou walk in thy way safely, and thy foot shall not stumble. When thou liest down, thou shalt not be afraid: yea, thou shalt lie down, and thy sleep shall be sweet* (Proverbs 3:23-24 KJV).

WORD OF ENCOURAGEMENT

It's easy to forget in the busyness of our lives that there are not only many Americans living and working overseas, but there are many of our fellow believers there. They are dedicated to offering compassion and assistance to countries less fortunate than ours. Gospel missionaries are deployed around the world fearlessly in the face of daily dangers in their heavenly assignment to preach salvation to the lost. Additionally, we also remember our valiant service men and women overseas and their families as well.

Nevertheless, we have seen times when Americans have been targeted by anti-American activists who hate this nation and want to destroy everything it stands for. Terrorists who seek to kill United States citizens have found their way into many nations once considered safe. It's certainly not a reason to fear international travel, but we must pray and prophesy for the safety of Americans abroad and particularly for our fellow believers assigned to and traveling in these places. It's a key part of decreeing God's blessing over our nation because the influence of our country reaches uniquely around the globe. We must use our faith for international safety and peace!

A CRY FOR FREEDOM AND DELIVERANCE!

DECLARATION

We decree that the freedom and liberty that marks this nation shall be kept sacred. We prophesy deliverance from every stranglehold that would restrict the ability for people to conduct their lives independently, soundly, decently, legally, and according to God's Word. We bind the spirit of the dictator and tyrant, in Jesus' Name. We break the advancement of socialists, communists, and fascists. We prophesy that they shall not steal the liberties enacted and sworn in by our founders. We say there is a freedom to enjoy life abundantly as God intends. We decree no laws shall be implemented that restrict Americans and Christians from following the Lord and the American dream. We declare a breaking to every law, mandate, and controlling measure that places unreasonable restrictions upon the fulfillment of life meant to be enjoyed by every human being. We declare non-compliance with wicked laws and demands. We say that every yoke of extreme and excessive governmental control shall be loosened. We say the authority of excessive tax demands and inquiries shall be overturned, and the rights of honest taxpayers shall be guarded. We decree no binding law shall be placed upon the Body of Christ, Christianity, the Bible, or the Church. We loose the spirit of freedom that is not according to the flesh, corruption, and immorality but is according to the liberty of Christ. We say the liberty that is found in salvation through Jesus shall reign supreme. We say a cry of freedom and deliverance shall arise in our land!

SCRIPTURE

The Spirit of the Lord is upon me, because he hath anointed me to preach the gospel to the poor; he hath sent me to heal the brokenhearted, to preach deliverance to the captives, and recovering of sight to the blind, to set at liberty them that are bruised (Luke 4:18 KJV).

I will walk about in freedom, for I have sought out your precepts (Psalm 119:45 NIV).

WORD OF ENCOURAGEMENT

God's Word reveals clearly that the Lord wants people set free. Jesus announced His mission, which is that He came to deliver captives and liberate the bruised and abused. Freedom is the cry in the heart of humanity, but the devil is the one who places the spirit of bondage inside people and incites them to enslave others some way. Satan is the one who raises up dictatorial leaders and tyrants who for personal gain choke out liberty.

Jesus wants people delivered from such bondage, but not so they can live in sin or revelry; rather, so they can lead a decent life that builds a future and a fulfilling legacy for their families extending to the upcoming generation. The United States has been a lighthouse of freedom around the world, and the devil has always been on the prowl to destroy that. We must raise up a cry to keep freedom paramount, and we must demand deliverance from all that currently binds our liberty in Jesus' Name!

PRAYER OF NATIONAL REPENTANCE

DECLARATION

We decree repentance from sin shall begin to arise across the United States of America. People everywhere shall turn from their wicked ways. Believers shall humble themselves from pride and begin to abhor evil. We say the Lord's Church shall seek Him like never before and ask Him to save our country. We declare there shall be a calling upon God for intervention, insight, and help. We bind the demonic forces of religious haughtiness, resistance, and rebellion among God's people, and we say they shall bow their knees in contrite humility. We prophesy that intellectualists who refuse instruction will not trample the efforts of those who desire God's grace and mercy to invade our land. We say that the repentant and meek shall inherit this nation. We declare the lost shall be saved because of the repentance within the Body of Christ and the Church. We decree that repentance shall miraculously impact governments, courts, businesses, schools, and families. People everywhere shall repent of immorality, sensuality, dishonesty, robbery, and their rejection of God. A calling out to the Lord shall organically and openly arise in cities, states, and regions. Even upon the media they shall say, "Great is our God!" because of the spiritual healing that God is bringing to our land. We say that there shall be a mass outpouring of repentance that shall descend upon the United States of America in Jesus' Name!

SCRIPTURE

> *If my people, who are called by my name, will humble themselves and pray and seek my face and turn from their wicked ways, then I will hear from Heaven, and I will forgive their sin and will heal their land* (2 Chronicles 7:14 NIV).

WORD OF ENCOURAGEMENT

God's Word is clear. For a nation to experience healing and blessing it begins with His people humbling themselves in repentance for their sin. It begins with us who know the truth and who know that the way for people to be saved is for them to turn from iniquity. We can't expect the world to repent when we ourselves remain unrepentant. Something supernatural takes place when the Church bows its knee in renewed humility before the Lord. We open the way for the unsaved to follow our example. The world also needs to see us postured in humility, something they are not versed in. The world is marked in pride, self-accomplishment, and selfishness. We can show them the way by our choice to place ourselves contritely under God's Almighty hand knowing we are nothing without His mercy and grace extended.

There have been many gatherings and calls for national repentance, and it's important to realize that many have responded. Many are repentant, crying out and trusting that God is hearing us. Let's believe there will be an ongoing cry for repentance that will be the key to the spiritual healing in our states and communities. A cry for national repentance is already happening, and it's shifting the United States of America in Jesus' Name!

BLESSING AND PEACE FOR ISRAEL

DECLARATION

We decree God's peace and blessing rests upon Israel and Jerusalem. We declare peace to her borders and that all enemy fire shall cease. We ask for angelic reinforcements to bring protection to the walls of Israel and that its places of government shall remain safe. We break the power of all dread, fear, and terror among the people. We say they shall not fear attacks, bombings, missiles, and foreign invasion. We prophesy that their homes, streets, businesses, and historical sites shall be protected. We declare that Israel's land shall remain secure, and no politicians or governments of the earth shall be able to enact agreements or accords that take their land away. We say that Jerusalem belongs to God. We speak strength to the state of Israel. We prophesy a prosperity from the Lord rests upon them and the Jewish people. We declare the Gospel of Jesus Christ shall shine in Israel and many shall come to the way of salvation. May the United States of America never break its alliance with Israel.

We bind every effort by the government to detach from Israel, and we declare that America shall always defend Israel and seek its good. We receive divine prosperity according to God's promise for loving Jerusalem, and we say that nothing shall interfere with our alliance. We decree Israel is blessed and Jerusalem is covered in peace, in Jesus' Name!

SCRIPTURE

> *Pray for the peace of Jerusalem: they shall prosper that love thee. Peace be within thy walls, and prosperity within thy palaces. For my brethren and companions' sakes, I will now say, Peace be within thee. Because of the house of the Lord our God I will seek thy good* (Psalm 122:6-9 KJV).

WORD OF ENCOURAGEMENT

When God told Abraham that He was making him a great nation, He said He would bless those who blessed him and curse those who cursed him (see Gen. 12:2-3). The nation of Israel as we know it was birthed from the offspring of Abraham through Isaac, and God has kept

Israel as the apple of His eye. There is no question that one of the reasons the United States has been blessed through the years is we have aligned with Israel and defended her interests. Countless Americans have involved themselves in seeking her good through efforts of compassion and humanitarian assistance.

It's been an understood matter that America aligns with Israel. Period. Of course, some political figures are trying to dilute that and become softened to Israel's foreign invaders. Our prayer needs to remain strong in declaring that our alliance with Israel will never be broken and that America will always defend her sovereignty and her borders. God has promised that when we seek for the good and peace of Israel, we will be blessed!

ABOUT
BRENDA KUNNEMAN

Brenda Kunneman is cofounder of One Voice Ministries and, with her husband, pastors Lord of Hosts Church in Omaha, Nebraska. She and her husband also host a weekly TV program, New Level with Hank and Brenda, on Daystar Television Network. Brenda is a writer and teacher who ministers nationally and internationally, preaching and demonstrating how to live life in the Spirit. Thousands visit her prophetic website: The Daily Prophecy. She has authored several books including: *Decoding Hell's Propaganda; Daily Decrees for Family Blessing and Breakthrough; Daily Decrees for Kids;* and others.

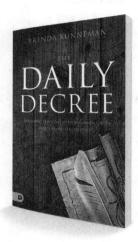

From
BRENDA KUNNEMAN

It's time for kids to decree God's Word over their lives!

Jesus said, "Let the little children come to me, and do not hinder them, for the kingdom of heaven belongs to such as these." — Matthew 19:14

Children don't have a junior Holy Spirit, nor are they secondary members of the Kingdom of God. They, too, have been given the right to be called Kings and Priests and their prayers and words carry authority in the spiritual realm.

Brenda Kunneman is a bestselling author and dynamic prophetic voice who has equipped believers around the world to boldly decree Heaven's victory over every area of their lives. Now she is equipping children with powerful, Bible-based, prophetic decrees that they can read and declare themselves!

These decrees are specifically designed to train children to operate in their heavenly authority, empowering them to engage the Kingdom that Jesus declared belongs to them!

As kids begin to boldly speak God's word, the same Spirit that raised Jesus from the dead releases heavenly power to see Kingdom decrees carried out! It's time for kids to decree God's Word over their lives!

Purchase your copy wherever books are sold.

From

Hank Kunneman

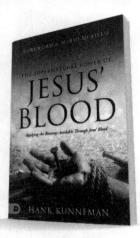

This prophetic revelation of the life-giving Blood of Jesus is critical in these precarious end-time days!

"And they overcame him by the blood of the Lamb, and by the word of their testimony; and they loved not their lives unto the death" (Revelation 12:11).

As believers in Christ, we are not immune to trouble. Challenges in areas like health, finances, jobs, and relationships come against us all. But Scripture shows us keys to our tremendous victory through Jesus' shed Blood!

Connecting both Old and New Testament principles, Hank Kunneman vividly highlights the prophetic revelation of Jesus' shed Blood and its overcoming power.

The Supernatural Power of Jesus' Blood will encourage you in:

·Understanding what is rightfully yours as a believer.
·Remembering God's faithfulness.
·Declaring your covenant promises.
·Pleading the Blood of Jesus over yourself and your loved ones.

Grab onto these prophetic truths and walk in the victory Jesus has provided through His shed Blood!

Purchase your copy wherever books are sold

YOUR Prophetic COMMUNITY

Are you passionate about hearing God's voice, walking with Jesus, and experiencing the power of the Holy Spirit?

Destiny Image is a community of believers with a passion for equipping and encouraging you to live the prophetic, supernatural life you were created for!

We offer a fresh helping of practical articles, dynamic podcasts, and powerful videos from respected, Spirit-empowered, Christian leaders to fuel the holy fire within you.

Sign up now to get awesome content delivered to your inbox
destinyimage.com/sign-up

 Destiny Image

From

Hank Kunneman

Receive the Father's heart and understand the power of Throne Room prophecy!

When it comes to prophecy, how can we discern if the words being spoken are true, false, or wrong? God is calling His people to press into a higher realm of revelation, so that the words they share come from Heaven, *not* from their flesh, soul, or other sources.

Hank Kunneman is a trusted father and mentor in the prophetic community. In this landmark book, he teaches you to speak prophetic words that carry thunder from Heaven's Throne Room! Learn to communicate messages from God with precision and accuracy—carrying the Father's heart as you carry His secrets.

In this timely book you will learn...

•To discern the three realms of information—the Earth realm, the occult realm, and the Throne Room realm.
•How prophetic words are important in the course of world events, in times of crisis, and in challenging times.
•To draw closer to the One seated on the Throne to increase intimacy necessary for prophetic accuracy.
•How "human filters" affect every prophet and prophecy.
•How to identify the characteristics of false *"horned"* prophets.

Now is the time to come up higher and receive the Father's heart and understand the power of Throne Room prophecy!

Purchase your copy wherever books are sold